Cambridge Elements

Elements in the Problems of God
edited by
Michael L. Peterson
Asbury Theological Seminary

MODELLING THE DIVINE

Ben Page
Eton College

Shaftesbury Road, Cambridge CB2 8EA, United Kingdom

One Liberty Plaza, 20th Floor, New York, NY 10006, USA

477 Williamstown Road, Port Melbourne, VIC 3207, Australia

314–321, 3rd Floor, Plot 3, Splendor Forum, Jasola District Centre,
New Delhi – 110025, India

103 Penang Road, #05-06/07, Visioncrest Commercial, Singapore 238467

Cambridge University Press is part of Cambridge University Press & Assessment,
a department of the University of Cambridge.

We share the University's mission to contribute to society through the pursuit of education, learning and research at the highest international levels of excellence.

www.cambridge.org
Information on this title: www.cambridge.org/9781009271004

DOI: 10.1017/9781009270991

© Ben Page 2025

This publication is in copyright. Subject to statutory exception and to the provisions of relevant collective licensing agreements, no reproduction of any part may take place without the written permission of Cambridge University Press & Assessment.

When citing this work, please include a reference to the DOI 10.1017/9781009270991

First published 2025

A catalogue record for this publication is available from the British Library

ISBN 978-1-009-70935-4 Hardback
ISBN 978-1-009-27100-4 Paperback
ISSN 2754-8724 (online)
ISSN 2754-8716 (print)

Cambridge University Press & Assessment has no responsibility for the persistence or accuracy of URLs for external or third-party internet websites referred to in this publication and does not guarantee that any content on such websites is, or will remain, accurate or appropriate.

For EU product safety concerns, contact us at Calle de José Abascal, 56, 1°, 28003 Madrid, Spain, or email eugpsr@cambridge.org

Modelling the Divine

Elements in the Problems of God

DOI: 10.1017/9781009270991
First published online: November 2025

Ben Page
Eton College
Author for correspondence: Ben Page, hi@ben-page.co.uk

Abstract: There are different approaches to modelling the divine, with each raising questions one needs to consider when employing them to produce a model. Outlining some of the most widely used methods is one of the goals of this Element, which provides something of an introductory 'how-to' guide for divine modelling. Through discussing what models are, the different sources of data acquisition, how to acquire data via reason, how to sort data, and what we might think a model provides us with, the Element aims to give readers the resources to take on the task of modelling informatively and effectively for themselves.

Keywords: divine, God, models, perfect being theology, creator theology

© Ben Page 2025

ISBNs: 9781009709354 (HB), 9781009271004 (PB), 9781009270991 (OC)
ISSNs: 2754-8724 (online), 2754-8716 (print)

Contents

1 Introduction 1

2 Why Model? 1

3 Sources of Data Acquisition 8

4 Acquiring Reason-able Data 16

5 Data Sorting 35

6 A Model Example 49

7 What Does a 'Divine' Model Actually Give Us? 56

Bibliography 63

the actual crime itself. Similarly, the Bohr model of an atom, which you learned about in school, represents certain features of a real atom. Yet, in both cases, these models are not the same as the reality they model in all respects. Rather, they merely provide us with a way of understanding some key features of the complex reality we are trying to understand by virtue of representing some features accurately. Models are therefore of primary use when something 'resists direct study, because it is so complex or hard to observe' (Williamson, 2022, 372).[7]

How then do models differ from the reality they represent?[8] This depends upon the *type* of model that is being employed, with there being a rich categorisation of different types of model within the philosophy of science (Frigg & Hartmann, 2020). For instance, *Toy Models* don't appear to represent much of the reality they are attempting to model since they are extremely simplified. *Idealised Models* also simplify complex reality in certain ways in order to make it more understandable. This idealisation can be accomplished by different means, such as through abstractly 'stripping away' aspects of the reality under consideration which are irrelevant to the goal of the model – so-called *Aristotelian Idealisation*, or by deliberately distorting the reality under consideration by idealising certain parameters – for instance by considering frictionless planes or perfectly rational and omniscient humans, which is known as *Galilean Idealisation*.[9] Finally, there are *Analogical Models*, which employ analogies to help us understand various phenomena, with the analogy either being the same as the phenomena in various ways, or just strongly resembling it.

As we shall see, we can find elements of these types of models in different approaches to modelling the divine. For instance, some may contend our model of the divine is so simplified that it's debatable whether it

---

[7] Here Williamson is speaking of 'systems' (2022, 372) and Weisberg talks of 'structures' (2016, 266–267). Yet whilst I take it that mathematical and logical models are paradigm types of models, I think there are other types of models too. For instance, models can be found in metaphysics (e.g. Paul, 2012), epistemology (Titelbaum, 2012; Greco, 2023, 6–39), ethics (Zagzebski, 2017, 5–6) – note that Zagzebski talks of 'theories' and 'maps', but her usage is very similar to my notion of a model), and philosophy of religion (e.g. Diller & Kasher, 2013), even though these are all different from purely mathematical and logical models.

[8] This way of speaking, although I shall employ it for ease of explication is slightly imprecise, for 'Models are not compared directly to real phenomena, but to target systems, which are abstractions over these phenomena' that the agent is specifically interested in (Weisberg, 2016, 267).

[9] In reality there are no such things as frictionless planes or perfectly rational and omniscient humans, although this later case ignores complications that arise from the Incarnation (Pawl, 2019, Part 3).

really can play any role in representing the divine at all. Others will suggest that our model of the divine often 'strips away' certain characteristics and merely focuses on others which are considered more important. Yet, others will contend that we perform a different type of idealisation in terms of stripping away arbitrary limits of the divine, and infinitising its attributes, with this apparently providing us with a more accurate model of the divine, rather than introducing inaccuracies into our model as it often does in scientific cases, and helps us finite beings better comprehend what the divine is like. And finally, some will suggest the best we can hope to do is represent the divine in terms of something like analogical language. Nevertheless, since models never perfectly represent the reality they are considering, it will be true to say that no model of the divine will perfectly represent the divine itself. It may also be that the data we employ when modelling the divine results in an underdetermination of models, such that multiple models seem to represent the divine just as well as others.[10] Our aim, therefore, in providing a good model of the divine is to provide a model or models that come the closest to representing the divine itself, albeit whilst acknowledging that they won't be able to do so perfectly.[11]

2.2 What Are Models?

Given this understanding of what models do, we can turn to another question: what ontological category do models belong to? Whilst some models can be *material* objects, it's clear the type of model I'm interested in here is not that, otherwise I might be subject to violating one of the Ten Commandments after all! Rather, the type of model I'll be working with is a *mental* object, with perhaps the dominant view holding these mental objects to be fictional or imaginary.[12] Yet that the models *themselves* are fictions doesn't mean that

---

[10] Kopersky (2015, 261) notes that this feature of models might be helpful when thinking about certain theological doctrines, such as the Atonement, suggesting that we see different 'theories' as incomplete, complimentary models of a complex theological truth which is ultimately inaccessible and perhaps incomprehensible to us.

[11] There is another, more extreme view one might take here, which is to claim that for some reason or another it is impossible to model the divine (for instance, see Jacobs (2015)). That is, it is not just hard for finite creatures to model the divine, but rather it is impossible for such creatures to comprehend what the divine is like, with the divine not being open to being represented by models. It may be, however, that modelling a greatest possible being, or something like this, is useful in other regards, even though this doesn't model the divine at all. The model we produce would model something that doesn't exist in mind-independent reality, even though the divine itself does (Wood, 2016).

[12] If the mind is material, then arguably the 'model' is material too, but I take it that this doesn't imply we'll commit blasphemy, as in the Golden Calf case, since worship shouldn't

what they attempt to model is itself fictional or imaginary, for in *most* cases what is modelled will be a part of mind-independent reality.

Relating this to modelling the divine, we can distinguish between realist and anti-realist views of the divine. Thus far I've spoken in a realist fashion and implied that there is some mind-independent reality which is represented by a model. But we could instead think in an anti-realist way, and thus hold that there is nothing that exists beyond the model in mind-independent reality, and therefore all there is the fictional mind-dependent model.[13] Whether we should be a realist or anti-realist about the divine is beyond the scope of this Element; however, what follows will be relevant whichever option we are partial to, since the models produced by both parties will often look the same. That is, both may take the same data and create a model of the divine in the same way, but whilst the realist will think that the model represents some mind-independent reality, the anti-realist will not.[14] Nonetheless, it does seem that the anti-realist will have an easier time on the whole, since their model does not need to represent or resemble something mind-independent in order to be a good model, whereas the condition of 'accurate representation' will need to be met for the realist. With all that said, to aid explication, for the remainder of the Element I'll speak in a realist way, albeit with the caveat that one could easily adapt much of what is said to an anti-realist view.

A further question might arise if we think of models as fictions, namely won't it be the case that what the model asserts is false, and therefore won't a fictional model of the divine be false as well? Proponents of the fiction view, however, needn't accept this result, since they can claim that

---

be directed towards a model but towards the divine (see Section 7.1). But what should be said of the prohibition of making idols in the Ten Commandments? Here we might think that if making a model of the divine is sufficient for making a material idol, then so too might be thinking about the divine – but surely that can't be right and so making a model shouldn't be problematic either. One could reply that there might be a difference in 'making' a model compared to merely thinking about the divine, with the 'making' being the problematic aspect. However, even if one does so, I think that so long as the model is not taken to be the divine (see Section 7.1), but at best an approximation of it, then we won't flout this commandment.

[13] For an influential anti-realist theistic view, see Cupitt (1980).
[14] It *may* be more complex than this, depending upon what an anti-realist takes models to be. For example, on views like Thomasson's (2020), when one creates a model, an abstract cultural artefact is produced which exists independently of the model's author. Thus, if an anti-realist theist adopted a position like this, the model of the divine would take on a life of its own once it was created, no longer merely being a mind-dependent entity, but rather a mind-independent abstract object.

fictions can and often do assert truths. Yet the worry about truth may rear its head in another way, in virtue of the fact that models merely *represent* or *resemble* reality, and therefore no model grasps the whole truth of that which it is attempting to model. Whilst this seems to be the case, models, as Williamson notes, can still provide us with 'vaguer truths of the general form "This model description fits the phenomenon better than that one does in the following ways," where the fit is usually approximate' (Williamson, 2022, 376). This is comparative knowledge, namely knowledge as to which model is superior when compared with others, and whilst we may have liked more than this from our model, in the case of the divine, I suspect we should be content with this level of knowledge. After all, it seems to me that we should heed the advice of Aristotle when he said that 'it is the mark of an educated person to look in each area for only that degree of accuracy that the nature of the subject permits' (1049b 24–26, translated by Crisp, 2014, 4–5) and remind ourselves that the subject of the divine nature is probably one of the most epistemically challenging subject matters to consider.

Additionally, understanding comparative knowledge to be the type of knowledge models give us is also helpful since it explains another phenomenon, namely why people often don't abandon a model at the first sign of some data that speaks against it. As Williamson recalls,

> A theoretical economist once remarked to me that a paper like Gettier's classic refutation of the analysis of knowledge as justified true belief by means of a couple of counterexamples … would be considered unpublishable in economics. For economics is primarily a model-building discipline: since no model is expected to fit the actual phenomena perfectly, pointing out that one fails to do so is not considered newsworthy. What defeats a model is not a counterexample but a better model, one that retains its predecessor's successes while adding some more of its own. (Williamson, 2022, 383)

To give an example more relevant to this Element's subject, something similar might be said for those who adopt a model of the divine which claims that the divine is perfectly loving even though they may possess bits of data that seem inconsistent with their model, namely lots of evil in the world. Equally, it seems to fit well with a process that often happens within theistic debates, where an aspect of the divine, say its omnipotence, may be remodelled in light of potential counterexamples, with a new model of omnipotence being preferred as it retains much of its predecessor's successes whilst adding some more of its own.

2.3 What Can Models Be Used for?

Once we've formulated a model, we might ask what it's useful for. Perhaps a primary use of models is employing them to gain additional knowledge (Weisberg, 2016, 264). In our case, in modelling the divine we will gain knowledge as to what is at stake if we go one way or another when producing our model. For instance, in building a model we may discover that if we take something as primary, it will constrain other parts of the model, such that we come to see that certain choices will produce certain models, whilst other choices will produce other models. Our model might also help inform us of other aspects of the divine which our current model doesn't explicitly contain, for instance by telling us that the divine must have other attributes of a particular type. Additionally, models of the divine *might* provide us with insight about other questions we may have, such as telling us what it is likely that the divine might do. For example, perhaps our model suggests it's very likely or even necessary that the divine creates, or maybe it tells us that we can have no epistemic access to the divine life whatsoever and therefore certain questions should be taken off the table.[15]

In any case, models of the divine often play a key role in answering other questions that are considered when philosophising about religion, with it often being the model of the divine that informs or determines the answers that are given. It is therefore vital that we have a good grasp on what we should think about when we construct a model of the divine so that we can formulate the best model we can.

2.4 A Modelling Framework

So far I've talked a lot about models and what they are, but this Element is not primarily about models of the divine. Rather, it's about modelling frameworks which concern the divine. The distinction here is that whilst a model is understood as a particular abstract representation of some target reality, a modelling framework provides us with a methodology or set of techniques for constructing this model (Titelbaum, 2012, 11; Greco, 2023, 9). This Element, then, is far more concerned with methodological questions to do with modelling the divine, rather than with giving a model of the divine itself. The first of these methodological

---

[15] For some recent discussion relating to the question as to whether the divine must create, see Buchak and Zimmerman (2022, chs. 7–13).

questions that we'll consider concerns the sources of data acquisition, and particularly those to do with how reliable we should think the data they produce is.

3 Sources of Data Acquisition

As a common quip has it, 'Data is like garbage. You'd better know what you are going to do with it before you collect it.'[16] Thankfully we know what we're going to do with the data we collect, namely use it to produce a model of the divine. But talk of 'garbage' might remind us of another popular saying, 'garbage in, garbage out'. In the context of modelling, this is important, for whilst data is needed in order to produce a model, if we use 'garbage' data to inform our model, the model we produce will be 'garbage' too. The aim of this section, therefore, is to consider questions of reliability that might be raised when thinking about different sources of data acquisition.

For the purpose of this Element, I'll assume there are four different ways that we can acquire data so as to produce a model of the divine: scripture, tradition, experience, and reason.[17] Whilst I suspect that some religious traditions may alter this list somewhat, perhaps through addition or subtraction, I think most will agree that all of these sources can provide some data. Nonetheless, each category brings with it questions to be answered, and we turn to some of these now.

3.1 Scripture

Arguably, many people will take scripture to provide much of the data to be employed when modelling the divine, for standardly, at least some scriptural texts describe the divine nature. Nevertheless, there are several questions we need to ask ourselves concerning how reliable and authoritative we should take this data to be.

An important question is the following: what is the influence or role of the divine in the production of the scripture under consideration? Some religious traditions will answer this by asserting that the divine's role is one of dictation, such that every word that is written is the word of the divine. Others, by contrast, hold to the other extreme, claiming that the divine played no role in the writing of these scriptures, leaving the writer wholly

---

[16] This quote is often attributed to Mark Twain, but it seems unlikely that he actually said such a thing. https://bit.ly/3IbRVHT.

[17] In Christian circles this is known as the Wesleyan quadrilateral. Note that here I speak of 'scripture' for ease, although it would be more accurate to understand this as 'purported scripture'.

...onally, many scriptures contain different genres throughout, and ... the way information about the divine nature is given will likely ... instance, even on the dictation view, the content one can gar... the divine nature through a narrative, even if wholly accurate, ... be very different from the content one would get through an ... history. Or, to take another example, data coming from texts of ... whilst sometimes seeming to be propositional, might also need ... erpreted as it may be considered exaggerated (Dunn, 1996, 93), ... primary purpose is to express praise and worship of the divine ... an accurately to describe its nature. The job of textual scholars ... fore be important in providing us with accurate data from scrip... it may be here that error, even for those who claim the text to ... ed, creeps in. For whilst the text may be dictated from a perfectly ... source, arguably none of those who interpret it do so with per... racy. This isn't to say that we can't or shouldn't employ data ... pture, but merely that we should be hesitant in thinking that if ... to a dictation understanding of scripture, modelling the divine ... and easy job. It might well be *easier* in providing reliable and ... tive data compared with the other views, but it is not without ... tions.

... briefly note two more difficulties that affect dictation, as well ... her views. The first concerns what it is that the divine wants to ... icate through scripture. It may have been that the divine most ... disclose how humans could achieve salvation, and yet in vir... ioritising this aim, it would have had to radically simplify the ... ion it disclosed about its nature. For suppose that salvation and ... e nature are inextricably linked, but that through disclosing the ... ture accurately the path to salvation would be inaccessible to finite ... ce they would fail to understand the accurate presentation of the ... ture and its repercussions for salvation.[22] However, if the divine ... radically simplify the explanation of its nature in various ways, ... ould provide a reliable and accessible guide to salvation which ... ngs could understand and follow. If something like this were the ... n it seems the divine would prioritise radical simplifications about ... rder to achieve its ultimate aim.[23] One might object, suggesting

---

some might stumble on it by accident, but they wouldn't know that they had.
at this also requires making certain assumptions about what the divine is like and would and wouldn't do, which again might be inappropriate given that we are at the data-gathering stage.

to their own devices. Finally, many adop
contend that the divine was in some way in
particular scriptures, but not by means of c
of the writers is also evident within the wri

It seems that a dictation view of script
most authoritative and accurate understa
words given to us are by the divine itself.[18]
thinking this only if we have an independe
divine is wholly reliable and trustworthy,
would be problematic, because even a liar
trustworthy. Additionally, supposing that
trustworthy means that one is already as
and since we are at the data-gathering stag
presuppose this model in order to ascertai
certain bits of data are. But suppose we'r
cerns, one might suppose that if a dictatio
the divine says about itself should be preser
if we could guarantee that we have the text
tated it, we shouldn't be too quick in appr
seems there are additional complications to

Firstly, it seems as though we're assuming
of propositions from which we can easily ex
it's far from clear that this is what the divir
Wright and Bird claim, 'The New Testamer
of propositional nuggets waiting to be orde
(Wright & Bird, 2019, 60). This is largely tr
it primarily giving us a big picture narrat
His people, telling of how He brings about
renewal.[20] Direct propositional content abo
not the norm. Therefore, all views of scriptur
will require further practices of interpretati
isn't obvious what the relevant 'data' from t

---

[18] Aquinas seems to agree with this, holding that the s
is based on divine authority (*Summa Theologica* I, c

[19] If Stump (2010) is right about how we acquire ':
importance of it, it might be that the divine gave us
information that couldn't be carried merely by prop

[20] See Bartholomew and Goheen (2014) for one way
narrative.

[21] How much work will be required will depend upon h
ture in question is.

that such a simplification would be unworthy of the divine. But note that this practice is often employed by those we take to be good teachers when helping students understand concepts they appear incapable of fully grasping. That is, radical simplifications might be made in certain areas to help the student increase their understanding of a more important idea, even if this will mean that ultimately they'll never be able to fully understand this idea or those that have been radically simplified. If they are incapable of this full understanding, then an increased understanding is the best we can hope for, and this may well be a trade-off the divine decides to make too. Since one can't be certain that this isn't the case, even if we adopt a dictation view, we should at least be open to the possibility that the data about the divine nature is radically simplified.

Finally, there is the question of whether human language is able to portray the divine nature accurately, for given that the scripture is addressed to a people of a certain time and place it must employ language that is understandable within that time and place. But perhaps this language, or any finite language, isn't developed enough to accurately portray the divine nature, even if the divine uses the best concepts that humans have at their disposal. Relatedly, even if the words that expressed the divine nature could do so in a wholly accurate manner, we would still need to ascertain the exact and correct meanings of these words, since the same words can express different meanings within different times and places, and one cannot guarantee that our contemporary understanding of the dictated words matches up with what the divine wished us to understand by these terms.[24] This question of language is one that will apply to any model of the divine more generally, unless we now have generated concepts that accurately represent the divine nature and which have no possible variation in meaning. Given this, we will need to think again about questions concerning language once we have produced our model.

Whilst these questions also apply to the intermediate view of scriptures, there are some additional questions to consider as well. For instance, we'll need to ascertain whether errors or inconsistencies are allowed within the text and if so, whether they are limited to some types of content or not. For instance, Hays writes that the New Testament 'is not a simple, homogeneous body of doctrine. It is, rather, a chorus of diverse voices. These voices differ not only in pacing and intonation but also in the material content of their messages. No matter how devoutly we might wish it otherwise, we

---

[24] Obviously, this can be mitigated by the work of textual scholars, who seek to uncover the meaning of the words the author had in mind when the text was written.

cannot hear these texts as a chorus speaking in unison' (Hays, 1996, 187).[25] On a dictation view these supposed inconsistencies may cause trouble for adopting the view itself, but for the intermediate view it may lead us to gather incompatible data about the divine. This might seem troublesome, but at this data-gathering stage we can just gather all the data we can and deal with inconsistencies later.

Additionally, the intermediate view will need to ascertain the relative value of the different bits of data garnered from scripture, for whilst on the dictation view all the bits of text will be dictated by the divine and will therefore be seemingly as authoritative as each other, this isn't the case for the intermediate view. Additionally, on the dictation view, the divine disclosing something *once* might be thought as good as the divine disclosing it multiple times, for although disclosing it multiple times might bring it to our attention more, something does not become more likely to have been dictated in virtue of being repeated. However, on the intermediate view we might think that the more something appears, the more likely it is that this was something the divine sought to inspire, especially if this is an idea propounded by multiple authors. At the very least it seems we should give prima facie preference to those ideas about the divine that appear more frequently and more widely. It may be that in reality the less frequent ideas are actually more accurate than the repeated ones, but given our epistemological outlook, thinking that frequency links with accuracy seems the best approach to take.[26]

Finally, if we take a non-inspired view of scripture, things are different, for on this view these texts are just the work of humans who describe their perceived interaction with the divine and/or other things that their religious tradition takes to be significant. Therefore, unless we have good reasons for thinking that the writers of these texts were able to provide more accurate information about the divine nature than others do with such experiences today, we might just classify this data under the umbrella of 'experience', since it might just be a historical accident that *these* experiences came to be important for the religious tradition rather than anything about the experiences themselves.

---

[25] A referee rightly points out that this quote doesn't require that there be 'errors' or 'inconsistencies', with my surrounding context implying that it should. However, Hays does seem to think there are inconsistencies in scripture (1996, 190, 192, n.7), even though he also thinks there can be unified scriptural positions on various subjects, even amid the diversity of scriptural voices.

[26] Much the same can be said regarding themes, or what Hays calls focal images (1996, 196), namely that inferences about what the divine nature is like drawn from these would seem more reliable than those drawn from less pervasive themes, since there is less data from which to draw such inferences.

3.2 Tradition

The data from tradition largely concerns those who have gone before and thought about the divine. Their ideas may have been codified into teachings of councils, written in books, or perhaps been passed down verbally or through culture as influential ideas. Different religious traditions hold different traditions to be authoritative for different reasons. This leads to an initial difficulty, namely working out which tradition(s) to follow and how to respond in cases of conflict between traditions. There is also the question of how valuable we should deem the data that tradition gives us. For instance, some Christians find the work of the 'Conciliar' councils to be authoritative and take what is said in these councils to provide us with data that we can reason directly from when thinking about the divine nature (Pawl, 2016; 2020). On the other hand, others think tradition is fallible and should always be weighed against other considerations, such as scripture (Bird & Harrower, 2019).[27] We might also ask what the role of the divine is in the production of these traditions, since this may help determine how authoritative we should think a particular tradition is. For instance, some think that certain traditions are inspired by the divine, whilst others think that the divine's involvement in tradition is always inferior to that of scripture, with the divine perhaps playing no role in the production of such traditions at all.[28]

Whatever one ends up thinking about the authoritativeness of tradition, one key benefit for at least some traditions (e.g. various Christian Creeds) is that this data includes explicit propositional content about the divine. However, this isn't true of all traditions, since some, such as the Hadith and Talmud will at times, like scripture, require some hermeneutical work to acquire propositional content.

The fact that tradition has usually been developed and refined over long periods of time by a group of impressive thinkers may also lend some prima facie weight to its claims, regardless of whether it has been inspired, and therefore we may think we should be cautious when going against this weight of thought. As Stump writes,

> On the other hand, although it is not guaranteed to be right, the cumulative consensus of a community of experts is more likely to be right than the views of one individual (or one small group) alone. From the

---

[27] This may lead to a difficulty concerning who decides which texts count as scripture, since it is tradition that is usually appealed to in order to answer this question.

[28] Tradition is also used by some to provide insight into how to read scripture and therefore it might be directly relevant to helping us ascertain what propositions we should think scripture seeks to express.

point of view of Christianity, while it is possible that God would allow his church to be deceived for centuries about what is true and essential to the faith, leaving the truth to be discovered centuries later by a lone individual or his group, the thought that God has actually done so isn't one that we should arrive at lightly. (Stump, 2023, 23)

3.3 Experience

People, both past and present, claim to have experiences of the divine. These experiences may be direct, where the divine is directly present, or indirect, where the divine is experienced via an intermediary being directly present. We might think that the data produced by direct experiences should be considered more reliable than the data produced by indirect experiences, since there is no intermediary that may distort what was experienced. This might be true, but it could be that the intermediary, when experiencing the divine, allows one to experience the divine in such a way that they are not overwhelmed by the experience, as one could be in a direct experience, and therefore they may be able to gain more perspicuous data from the indirect experience.

Experiences of the divine can also refer to one's own experience, or the experience of others, and here one may think that one's own personal experiential data about the divine is more valuable than the data we gain from other people's experiences. Yet it's not clear that this is the case, especially if one's own experience is inconsistent with the experience of many others.[29]

Whatever we end up thinking about this experiential data and which type, if any, is to be preferred, many will conclude that experience can provide us with some data about the divine, since just as our experience more generally provides us with data about external phenomena, our experience about the divine can provide us with data about this entity too.[30] However, one might raise concerns about its reliability. For one, various people appear to have different and sometimes seemingly incompatible experiences of the divine, where one's psychological state and cultural surroundings often appearing to influence their experience. There are also

---

[29] Yet this isn't foolproof either, since sometimes it's likely that the rational thing to do is prefer your experiential data over numerous contradicting experiential data that is given by others.

[30] Endorsing phenomenal conservatism more generally may lead to this conclusion, with it holding that if it seems to you that x is the case then in the absence of any defeaters you have some justification for thinking x is the case. For some recent discussion on the reliability of religious experience see Oppy and Pearce (2022, 65–89; 232–237, 249–254, 292–297).

cases where people with psychosis claim to experience the divine, and even if we respond by saying that their experience is produced by a deviant causal chain, such that it is not caused in an 'appropriate' way, the fact that there can be deviant causal chains in relation to the divine might make us question whether the other experiences of the divine are also deviant. Additionally, we finite beings may just not be well suited to produce accurate data about the divine from our experiences, perhaps in virtue of our finite capacities and limited reasoning abilities, with these limitations being less troublesome when it comes to experience providing us with data about everyday finite reality.[31] Finally, there is the recurring issue of how we can ascertain the relevant propositional content, since experience is not directly propositional. This is made even more difficult as many who experience the divine give seemingly paradoxical descriptions of the experience and sometimes suggest that the experience itself is wholly indescribable. However, this itself may provide us with some data concerning the divine, namely that it is a vain hope to think we can produce anything like a wholly accurate model of it.

3.4 Reason

The final way we can acquire data about the divine is through using our reason or intellect. In some sense the use of reason has been apparent in each of the other ways of gathering data, helping us to understand and interpret words of scripture, enabling us to formulate traditions, and empowering us to interpret and evaluate experiences. Nonetheless, one's reason can be used more directly, but before commenting on how this is done, let me note some more general questions about using this source to acquire data.

The biggest concern regarding reason is to do with how reliable we should think its deliverances are, with this being more important for that data which relies directly on it. Instances of peer disagreement might suggest that our reasoning abilities aren't perfectly reliable, since two well-informed people with the same arguments and data can come to very different conclusions.[32] Reason is also sometimes easily affected by other aspects of our mental lives, such as emotion, peer pressure, and so on, and therefore we might think we can't fully trust what it produces. Additionally, there is the

---

[31] Our finite abilities may, however, still cause us problems in thinking about very complex aspects of reality, which is often a reason why we turn to 'models' in the first place.

[32] This happens all the time in philosophy – think of debates concerning free will, ethics, personal identity, etc. For a recent example in philosophy of religion see Oppy and Pearce (2022).

worry that our reasoning abilities, as powerful as they may be, are still finite and limited, and so if the divine is infinite and unlimited, any data they produce regarding the divine won't be wholly accurate. Finally, reasons based on religious traditions might be given for thinking that reason can't produce accurate data about the divine, with some perhaps holding, like Barth (*Church Dogmatics* I/1 §8.2, 2010, 26), that the intellect is fallen to such an extent that reason cannot grasp what the divine is like, or perhaps alternatively, that the intellect, although not fallen, doesn't have the capacity to bridge the divide between Creator and Creature.[33]

Whether there are good answers to these questions and those raised regarding the other sources of data acquisition will be important for ascertaining which sources do provide us with data about the divine and which sources should be prioritised. For the purposes of this Element, I'm going to assume these concerns can be overcome and that useful data can be acquired from all the sources I've spoken of here. Exactly how this is to be done for each would require much more discussion, with the details likely requiring knowledge that is beyond my area of expertise, and therefore I turn to discuss how to gather data from the source philosophers claim to know best, namely reason. However, this isn't to say that the other sources of data acquisition won't reappear in this Element, since they will later on when we think about data sorting and when I provide an example of how to go about modelling the divine.

4 Acquiring Reason-able Data

Sherlock Holmes once said, 'It is a capital mistake to theorize before one has any data' ('A Scandal in Bohemia'; Doyle, 2022, 157). How then do we acquire data which we can use to model the divine from reason? Outlining some of the most popular approaches for doing so is the aim of this section. However, before diving into this, let me note that the data gathered here typically concerns what is essential and intrinsic to the divine nature rather

---

[33] For some critical discussion of this type of concern see Wood (2021, ch. 6). In a personal communication (2025), Tim Pawl provided a response a Christian could use against Barth. He writes, 'If Barth is right, and we cannot tell what God is like outside of God's self-revelation, then there could be two contenders for being God incarnate, Jesus and David Koresh, and we couldn't rule either out by his actions on earth. After all, his actions on earth are the actions of God, and we can't tell what God would be like aside from God's divine testimony – which we get through that very guy! So the fact that David Koresh did those wicked sexual things does not count against his alleged divinity. But of course it does! So we can use outside sources – like our own sense of morality, our own arguments for the impermissibility of certain deplorable acts, etc – as conditions on what God is like.'

than what is contingent and extrinsic to it,[34] or in other words, what is invariant to the divine across all possible worlds.[35] This isn't to say that the divine has no contingent or extrinsic properties, for it may well, but rather that the methods used here don't necessarily tell us about these.[36] With that in mind let's turn to perhaps the most famous philosophical methodology for acquiring data about the divine, namely perfect being theology (PBT).[37]

4.1 Perfect Being Theology (PBT)

Anselm is probably the most well-known advocate of PBT, but he is far from the first adopter, with it arguably being employed by Plato, Aristotle, Zeno, Cicero, Augustine, and Boethius (Leftow, 2011, 104–106, 112–113).[38] PBT stems from the thought that the divine should be defined, at least partially, in terms of being a perfect being (PB), and that there can be no being which is greater, since nothing can be greater than that which is perfect. We can think of this as a type of idealisation, which (as we saw in Section 2.1) is a practice useful in producing models in that it strips away any other potential aspects of the complex reality we are modelling, in this case the divine, and focuses on a key aspect of it, namely its perfection. This *is not* to suggest that what is produced via PBT is necessarily inaccurate, since the divine seems to be the primary candidate for a PB and so the idealisation in terms of perfections is appropriate here, but it may only provide us with a partial account of what the divine nature is like since it could include more than that which can be grasped through thinking about perfection alone.[39]

Therefore, supposing we accept the divine to be a PB, how does PBT work? Typically, it does so in two stages. The first – the data acquiring stage – attempts to work out which perfections, or attributes, a PB *might* have, whilst the second – which we'll call the data sorting stage – works on

---

[34] Exactly what is meant by intrinsic is a tricky business, but for some discussion see Rubio (2025).
[35] Note that what is discussed in this section is different from the intrinsic probability of the divine (Miller, 2018), although the model we produce may have implications for this.
[36] It might be that some of the methods spoken of here can give us information about contingent features of the divine. For instance, some forms of creator theology (CT) might tell us that the divine has created. But other methods, such as PBT, arguably do not provide us with such information (Leftow, 2023, 171–172).
[37] The sections on PBT are indebted to Brian Leftow's lecture series on PBT as well as conversations with him about the topic as well. For more, see Leftow (forthcoming a).
[38] For some discussion of Anselm's specific approach see Leftow (2004).
[39] Therefore, it's incorrect to think that PBT must only be a '*single divine-attribute* (SDA) doctrine' (Zarepour, 2022, 5; italics original), since PBT is compatible with the divine possessing other fundamental attributes which cannot be grasped through consideration of perfection.

forming a consistent set of perfections so as to formulate the notion of a PB (Leftow, 2012, 9–10).[40] Since this section is focused on acquiring data, whilst the following is on data sorting, I'll concentrate only on stage one here and leave stage two for later.

4.1.1 PBT Stage One: Acquiring Potential Perfections

There are different ways in which PBT might attempt to ascertain perfections that the divine may possess. The first – the 'a priori method', or 'armchair method' – does so by a priori means (Leftow, 2015, 424; 2011). To avoid any confusion, let me note that talk of 'a priori' here *does not* mean that we rule out experience as being required in order to acquire and understand the concepts PBT considers. Rather, a priori-PBT supposes that given various concepts, one can work out via reason alone what perfections a divine being possesses.[41] A priori-PBT therefore suggests that the question we need to ask is whether some candidate attribute is better to have than to lack. If this candidate attribute is better to have than to lack, then this provides us with some reason for thinking that this is a perfection a PB possesses. To take an example, suppose we consider the divine's epistemic attributes, and in particular the ability to know truths and avoid falsehoods. This attribute seems better to have than to lack, and so we have some reason to think it's an attribute a PB possesses. However, it's also clear that we have not considered the perfect version of this attribute yet, since surely a PB would be more likely to possess a perfect rather than imperfect version. To ascertain what the perfected attribute is we will therefore need to deny any imperfections associated with the attribute in question, with this *usually* denying that there are any limits to the attribute.[42] As such, in the case we are considering, the relevant question about the

---

[40] I speak of attributes, but this isn't meant to imply any sort of metaphysical picture as to what attributes are. As such, I take it that what I say here is compatible with strong versions of divine simplicity, something Anselm himself endorsed (e.g. *Monologion* 17, and *Proslogion* 18), and/or claims to the effect that PBT only provides us with language that is appropriate for describing the divine, a claim Anselm also endorsed (Leftow, 2004, 134), rather than some metaphysically robust conception of its nature.

[41] Thanks to Brian Leftow for helping me see this. See Kitcher (1980; 2000) for an account of a priori that fits with this. In light of this understanding, those, such as Mawson (2019), who use experience when thinking about PBT, can still be considered as endorsing a priori-PBT so long as experience is just used in order to acquire and understand the various concepts PBT considers, with reason then determining from these concepts which are those that a PB possesses.

[42] Again, this is a type of idealisation, although this isn't to imply that this idealisation brings with it inaccuracies in describing a PB, since it might provide the most accurate way of describing such a being given that we are finite beings with limited intellectual powers.

perfected attribute will be whether it is better to have or lack the ability to know *all* truths and avoid *all* falsehoods. It is this perfected attribute, which cannot be improved upon, that we have some prima facie reason for thinking a PB would have. Note, however, that whilst it might be that the perfect form of an attribute is often one which denies any limit to the attribute, I think it would be a mistake to therefore conclude that PBT can only license attributes that come in degrees, contra Kvanvig (2021, 115) and Murphy (2017, 19). This is because all PBT requires is that the attribute in question is better to have than to lack, and it may be that some non-degreed attributes are better to have than to lack and therefore can be considered perfections that we have prima facie reason for thinking a PB possesses.

One consideration which leads us to think that we only get prima facie support for a PB possessing this attribute is because the attribute in question might turn out to be what is called a *mixed* or *impure* perfection, namely a perfection that brings along with it some type of imperfection. If it doesn't bring an imperfection with it, then we can call this type of attribute a *pure perfection*, and it is these *pure perfections* that are the *primary* data we want PBT to deliver.[43] Exactly what counts as a *mixed* and by extension *primary* perfection may, however, be somewhat controversial and person dependent. Historically, many examples of *mixed* perfections were those perfections which brought with them materiality, since matter was taken to be limiting in some way. However, given that some conceptions of the divine claim that the divine is material, there are those who might not find materiality problematic. They may instead find that thinking of divine as immaterial raises more issues, perhaps to do with supposed implications of the divine being either too distant or unable to interact with creation. For present purposes, whether this is correct is neither here nor there, but what it does demonstrate is that if one wishes to claim that a perfection is *mixed* or *pure*, further work will have to be done demonstrating the entailments of the perfection. To give another example, some might claim that impassibility is a *mixed* perfection since whilst it may be a perfection to depend upon nothing, it supposedly brings with it the imperfection of lacking empathy. By contrast, others might think passibility is a mixed perfection since whilst it implies that the divine can exhibit empathy, it also requires that the divine is in some way dependent on something outside of itself.[44] Obviously here, arguments will need to be given as to why

---

[43] Scotus was aware of this distinction, see Wolter (1987, 172, n.14).
[44] Here I am just assuming for the sake of argument that impassibility and passibility have these implications.

empathy and independence are perfections, and why impassibility prevents empathy and passibility flouts independence. Supposing a person were to find some of these arguments unpersuasive, then it may be that they would suggest that (when properly understood) one of these attributes is in fact a *pure* perfection rather than a *mixed* one.[45] Nonetheless, this isn't to say that the divine can exhibit no *mixed* perfections, since they *may* characterise our notion of a PB if these attributes are compatible with the *pure* perfections.[46] However, as determining their exact role and whether they should be ruled out entirely is tricky, it is the *pure* perfections that we should take to be the initial candidates when thinking about what a PB is like.

Given all this talk of 'perfection', one might wonder what it means to be 'perfect', since it appears that talk of 'perfection' presupposes some type of objective 'value' from which we can judge that some attribute is a *pure* perfection.[47] Note also that this 'value' isn't something that is limited to ethical value, as should be evident from our example above. 'Value' here concerns epistemic value and norms, as it is from this type of value that we can conclude that knowledge is better than error, and having all knowledge and no error is the most perfect epistemic state to be in.[48] Yet whilst it's clear what type of value we're appealing to in some cases is, in others it is less so. For instance, PBT might suggest that there is a *pure* perfection regarding power, but what scale of value are we appealing to when we consider whether power is preferable to non-power, and which degree of power is most perfect?[49]

Here it seems we have two options before us. The first (and perhaps more common) view would be that there is such a thing as perfection *simpliciter*, with *simpliciter* here implying that perfection has no qualification or condition and therefore is not relative to a kind, and that perfection *simpliciter* provides us with an ultimate scale of value.[50] Alternatively, one could say that 'kind' membership is what supplies us with a scale of value in this case, and therefore the kind a PB belongs to determines what it is to

---

[45] Adams (1999, 31) provides an example of a *mixed* perfection that I think most would accept, namely cuteness.
[46] These impure perfections might also be confirmed by our other data acquisition methods.
[47] Kvanvig writes, 'regardless of the precise character of PBT endorsed, it presupposes an objective value theory' (2021, 8).
[48] There would likely be more to it than just this, such as something to do with how and to what extent this knowledge is justified, etc.
[49] For instance, whilst omnipotence might be what some take to be the perfect degree of power, many process and feminist theologians would disagree.
[50] Hill (2005, 1–26) often calls this greatness *simpliciter*.

be a perfect instance of that kind. Interestingly, these two options parallel another debate concerning the nature of goodness, in which Plato held to a notion of goodness *simpliciter* whereby all things could be ranked by this ultimate scale of value, whilst Aristotle claimed that goodness is 'fractured' and therefore dependent on kind membership.[51] Let us therefore think about each of these options in turn.

From Anselm's writing, it seems that he was an advocate of the perfection *simpliciter* approach, for he wrote,

> Now [some things are such that] it is in every respect better to be _____ than not-_____, for example, wise than not-wise: that is, it is better to be wise than not-wise. … Indeed, whatever is not-wise in an unqualified sense, insofar as it is not-wise, is less than what is wise, since everything that is not-wise would be better if it were wise. … By contrast, [some things are such that] it is in some respect better to be not-_____ than to be _____: for example, not-gold than gold. For it is better for a human being to be not-gold than gold, even though perhaps it would be better for something—say, for lead—to be gold than not-gold. … As for everything else, if each is considered individually, either _____ is better than not-_____, or not-_____ is in some respect better than _____. Therefore, just as it is impious to think that the substance of the supreme nature is something that it is in some way better not to be, so he must be whatever it is in every respect better to be than not to be. For he alone is that than which absolutely nothing else is better, and he alone is better than all things that are not what he is. (Monologion, ch. 15 – Williams, 2007, 22–23)

From this passage it's clear that Anselm has in mind some type of *simpliciter* value, which is broader than merely ethical and epistemic value whilst also not being relative to a kind. But what, we might ask, makes gold intrinsically more valuable than lead? Historically we might have made this judgement based on the idea that there is a great chain of being, such that all of reality is hierarchically structured and includes corresponding differences in value. But this assumption is one that many today don't embrace.[52] We also don't seem able to say that the divine determines what has *simpliciter* value in the sense that it decrees that gold is intrinsically more valuable than lead, since this would appear to lead us into a bootstrapping worry. After all, this *simpliciter* value is meant to characterise the divine's intrinsic nature as well, and therefore the divine is too 'late' to determine this value scale.

---

[51] For a discussion of the debate between Plato and Aristotle see Shields (2024).
[52] For further discussion see Nagasawa (2017, 40–76). For a recent attempted partial revival of the great chain of being see Oderberg (2022).

However, perhaps we don't need to answer this question, and instead say that all we need to be able to do to conduct PBT is to accurately gauge what is perfect *simpliciter*, since from this we can work out which attributes are more valuable than others. Hill thinks we can do something like this primarily through thinking about 'various examples and thought experiments' (2005, 5). Yet the example he provides for suggesting that we understand 'greatness *simpliciter*' relates to ethical value (Hill, 2005, 23) rather than the seemingly 'ontological value' (Leftow, 2011, 109) that we'd be concerned with when thinking about questions such as whether unlimited power is a perfection. We might also be sceptical of the idea that examples and thought experiments can provide us with accurate knowledge regarding what counts as perfect *simpliciter*, since it's far from clear that everyone has the same intuitions about what perfections are. For instance, when conducting PBT, Murphy (2017; 2021, 84–98) and Leftow (2013; 2019) come to starkly different conclusions about what it means for the divine to be morally perfect or good, with this partially stemming from different ideas as to what perfection is. This disagreement doesn't force us to say there's no such thing as perfection *simpliciter*, for it may be that some are mistaken as to what this perfection is, but it should at least give us a reason for lowering our credence in our conclusions about what counts as perfection *simpliciter*.[53] As Leftow says elsewhere,

> As I give ... [PBT arguments] I have a nagging fear that I am making stuff up. This is not due to uncertainty about God's being perfect. Rather, our ideas of what it is to be perfect are inconsistent and flawed, and there is no guarantee that they match up with what God's perfection actually is. (2012, 11–12)

Leftow doesn't think that this means we shouldn't engage in this type of inquiry, since he thinks there are similar concerns regarding metaphysical inquiry more generally, and insofar as we continue to have some reason to proceed with metaphysical inquiry we should do the same with PBT.[54] Much the same could have been said for pretty much any area of philosophy, since the reliance on intuition is fairly rampant. As such, reaching different conclusions because one has different intuitions about a particular line of reasoning is usually the norm. Perhaps an advocate of the *simpliciter* approach can make this view more appealing by providing

---

[53] This is similar to certain debates in ethics about whether one should be a moral realist (Huemer, 2005, 128–154).

[54] Admittedly, Leftow himself doesn't opt for a perfection *simpliciter* or a priori form of PBT, and so he might think these concerns are more grave for this form of PBT.

a plausible epistemological theory so as to suggest how we have reliable access to the notion of perfection *simpliciter*, maybe giving an account that is similar to how intuitionists think we gain access to non-natural ethical truths (Huemer, 2005, 99–127), or by telling a story about how our cognitive faculties are generally reliable in matters concerning perfection, possibly by adapting Plantinga's (2000) in order to explain why a divine being wouldn't want us to be invariably mistaken on this matter. In any case, these are some of the challenges the *simpliciter* approach must overcome.

By contrast, the kind membership approach doesn't endorse a notion of perfection *simpliciter*, instead taking perfections to be relative to kinds, with the kind itself determining what it is for something to be a perfect instance of its kind.[55] This approach seems less epistemologically challenging so long as we have a way of ascertaining what kind the divine belongs to and what the perfections of that kind are, both of which may themselves be difficult tasks. There are other issues with this view as well. For one, it still seems that there will be some type of hierarchy of value between kinds and how we can make sense of this will need explaining. To see this, suppose there are two beings of different kinds which exhibit all the perfections their kinds permit and to their maximal degree. However, note that the first being exhibits fewer perfections in total when compared to the second being. Plausibly, one might say that because of this, the second being is more perfect than the first, and we might further claim that the kind the second being belongs to is more perfect than the first too. On the other hand, we might plausibly come to a different judgement –for it could be that some of the perfections the first being exhibits seem superior to those of the second, even though the total number it exhibits are less, and so we may wish to say that the first being, and perhaps its kind too, is more perfect than the second. But in either of these cases, if we are going to say any of this, then it won't be kind membership that is enabling us to say it; rather, it seems we will be appealing to some kind of *simpliciter* notion of perfection and all the issues that come along with it.[56]

Speaks raises another issue for the kind account when he writes, 'If we choose the kind-relative notion, then some choices of a kind seem to give the wrong results, whereas others (e.g. the kind deity) seem to presuppose

---

[55] Leftow (2012, 301) and Kvanvig (2021, 8), for instance, when thinking about PBT speak about the PB being of the kind 'deity', although Leftow thinks 'deity' is plausibly a subkind of 'person'.

[56] Perhaps one could say that both beings belong to a higher kind, but for this to work we'd likely end up with something similar to a great chain of being, which as I've already noted, is by no means a popular notion.

a knowledge of the divine nature that we might have wanted perfect being theology to provide rather than presuppose' (2014, 258). The problem here is that we had employed PBT to provide us with a greater understanding of the divine nature, and yet if we make sure we attribute the right kind to the divine, e.g. deity, then it seems we are already building into the process of PBT what we think the divine is like, rather than using it as a way of generating new information about the divine. One reply here might be to suggest that the kind in question doesn't need to be as specific as deity but could instead be something like a person (Leftow, 2015, 242).[57] But if we are to adopt this, we'll need good grounds for thinking that the divine is a person, especially since some writings on PBT don't think that PBT will imply that personhood is a perfection (Kvanvig, 2021, 80–85).[58]

Finally, at least historically, the option based on kind membership hasn't been widely embraced since many have wanted to say that the divine doesn't belong to any kind (e.g. Aquinas, *Summa Theologica* I, q.3, a.5). In fact, Scotus's *mixed* or *impure* perfections are sometimes interpreted as referring to those perfections that are relative to a kind, rather than those that are perfect *simpliciter* (Murphy, 2023). Here one might push back and say that every being belongs to a kind, given how we are understanding 'kind', since all it means to suggest is that the being in question has an essence, and that some beings may have the same 'kind' of essence. Even Aquinas (*Summa Theologica* I, q.3, a.2 & a.3) thinks the divine has, or more precisely is, an essence, and that only the divine alone exhibits this 'kind' of essence. Perhaps a reply built along these lines would suffice here.

However, there are more radical routes one could take when thinking about PBT, for whilst we've been looking for a way of making sense of an objective notion of perfection, we could claim that the notion of perfection is entirely subjective and that looking for an objective base is misguided. If we go along this route, then there are two ways one might think about what we're doing. First, we might claim that *we* cannot in principle

---

[57] Thinking of the divine as a person often plays a significant role in PBT, but this isn't to say that all who provide models of the divine find attributing personhood to the divine plausible (Bishop & Perszyk, 2023; Gasser & Kittle, 2022). By this I don't really mean to refer to discussions of so-called 'classical theism' and 'theistic personalism', since their disagreement concerning whether the divine is a person often seems overblown (Page, 2019; Wood, 2021, ch. 9), especially compared with more obviously a-personal views.

[58] This isn't to suggest they are right, after all Kvanvig's reservations largely come from thinking PBT can supply perfections which concern gradable attributes (2021, 82), something I've already said I think is mistaken. However, even if one agrees with Kvanvig, Mawson (2019, 15–20) suggests personhood is degreed, and thinks there are good PBT reasons for thinking a PB is a person.

apprehend the objective nature of perfection, and that although the divine is objectively perfect, we ultimately can have no idea what this entails. Yet we might still think the data we acquire from PBT has some value, especially if we have a low view of the data gathered from other sources. If we adopt the more general opinion that we cannot really know about the divine, then we might still say that the perfections we attribute to it are important in the context of worship, since the divine can be thought of as worthy of worship in virtue of its being perfect, even if the perfections we represent it as possessing are merely our subjective takes (rather than its actual objective perfections). Alternatively, one might claim that there is no objective nature to perfection at all, and that all talk of perfection is subjective. If we adopt an anti-realist view of the divine, we may nonetheless say that the perfections PBT gives us are still useful, once again in the context of worship, even though all we're doing is applying our subjective notions of perfection onto this non-existent entity. However, if we do take either of these routes, we'll need to be clear that we are explicitly modelling the divine in *our* image of perfection, although the reason why we do this will vary across the two views.

I think it's safe to say that most advocates of PBT would find either option too radical. However, there are different routes one could take instead. To see this, note that so far, we've been thinking about PBT as providing a new a priori method of data acquisition about the divine – but we don't have to think about it in this way. For instance, PBT could be used to give us a priori reasons in *support* of a religious tradition we take to be authoritative, thereby further confirming the data we had acquired from the religious tradition, perhaps in part or in full, rather than supplying new and distinct data itself.[59] Alternatively, we could adopt what Leftow endorses, namely scriptural-PBT (2011; 2012, 7–12; 2015, 424), where the role of PBT is to further explicate data that is given to us by authoritative sources, such as certain scriptures. On this way of conducting PBT, we start from the conception of the divine given in scripture and use perfect-being thinking merely to flesh it out (Leftow, 2015, 424). Scriptural-PBT is therefore not a priori in the sense of giving a priori reasons for thinking the divine possesses a particular perfection, nor does it provide confirmation of prior data; rather, it expands upon other data we have acquired through elaborating on its content. One benefit of scriptural-PBT, as Leftow notes, is that it

---

[59] One can infer from what Anselm says about the *Monologion* in the prologue to the *Proslogion* (Williams, 2007, 75–76) that this is likely what he was up to. My thanks to Brian Leftow for bringing this to my attention.

does not deal in such notions as perfection of being, perfection *simpliciter* or greatness *simpliciter*. It has no need of these because it begins from 'thick' descriptions of God and tries only to make them thicker; it does not seek to warrant the initial 'thick' descriptions by reference to these allegedly more fundamental notions. This is an advantage, as these notions are opaque. (2011, 108)

As such scriptural-PBT can likely overcome some of the issues I've discussed above, albeit at the expense of no longer being able to provide us with an independent source for thinking that some candidate perfection is one that the divine likely possesses.

PBT, depending upon how it's done, may therefore be able to provide us with either some new data for modelling the divine, in particular *pure* perfections, or an additional reason for thinking data gathered from another source is either reliable or can expand on data acquired from a distinctive source. Additionally, we might think that it can provide us with more data in virtue of the derivations we can make in light of considering various perfections, such as if the divine has pure perfection x, and x implies y, then the divine has y too. All of this can therefore be added to our data set, ready to be sorted later.

4.2 Creator Theology (CT)

Another way of acquiring data about the divine via reason sometimes goes by the name of creator theology (CT) (Kvanvig, 2021, 8–19). One way to understand this methodology is by thinking of it as coming to conclusions about the divine nature which are based on successful arguments within natural theology.[60] On this way of thinking about things, what CT is interested in is what is sometimes called 'stage II' of the natural theological process, where one attempts to show that what has been concluded to is divine, rather than 'stage I', which merely concludes to some thing or other which one hopes can ultimately be categorised as divine.[61] It's therefore important to notice that CT has a metaphysical starting point, namely that metaphysical entity which is concluded to exist at the end of 'stage I' of the natural theological process, such as a being which is the source of all contingent reality, and it is from this metaphysical starting point that we can think about the data we can acquire about the intrinsic nature of this

---

[60] The natural theological arguments I am referring to are those which do not rely on ideas of 'perfection' for arguing to the existence of the divine, so not ontological arguments which Leftow thinks are likely more accurately called 'arguments from perfection' (2005a, 80), since these are linked to PBT.

[61] For more on this distinction see Rasmussen (2010).

entity.[62] Alternatively, CT can be thought of as starting from a different definition of the divine than the one PBT starts with, this time claiming that the idea of ultimacy, or source of all, is what the divine, if it exists, is like. Nonetheless, whichever option one takes, what CT asks is, given that the divine can be understood as something like the source of all contingent reality, what type of being will be required to play that role, for in answering that question we'll acquire more data regarding the divine.

What, then, can we conclude about a being which is the source of all contingent reality?[63] The answer may well depend upon one's background metaphysical assumptions. To see this, suppose we think a reason we have for arriving at this metaphysical starting point is that we take Aquinas's first and most manifest way to be successful (*Summa Theologica*, I, q.2, a.3, co.). Let's assume, therefore, that everything contingent is in motion, so to cover all contingent reality, and conclude, along with Aquinas, that there is a first mover that is an immovable mover. Given Aquinas's metaphysical assumptions regarding motion, what we more precisely can conclude to is a being that is pure actuality with no potentiality, since for Aquinas, something is in motion insofar as it goes from being potentially x to actually x, and therefore an immovable mover is a being that is in no way potential and in every way actual.[64] Yet this metaphysical backdrop allows Aquinas to infer a number of different things about the divine. Firstly, Aquinas argues that a purely actual being must be simple, since for him, all composites are composite in virtue of being in some way composed of potentiality and actuality. Yet since we've concluded to a being that is pure actuality, it cannot be a composite in any way (*Summa Theologica*, I, q.3). Using another metaphysical assumption, namely that something is perfect insofar as it is actual, Aquinas argues that a being that is pure act must be wholly perfect (*Summa Theologica*, I, q.4). From this, and employing the ideas of pure actuality, simplicity, and perfection, Aquinas derives many of the other standard attributes of the divine, ultimately providing a fairly expansive amount of data as to what the divine is like.[65] *But* we will only find this data valuable insofar as we agree with

---

[62] CT is therefore not concerned with the epistemological question as to how and whether we can know that such a being exists (Kvanvig, 2021, 10–11).

[63] What exactly counts as a 'contingent reality' and whether the divine should be considered the source of any of necessary reality is something that has been debated. See Leftow (2012) and Gould (2014).

[64] For a sympathetic discussion of Aquinas's first way as well as his metaphysical background see Feser (2009, 65–81).

[65] See Leftow (2023, 171) for more on Aquinas and perfection, and De Haan (2023) for more on Aquinas's overall methodology.

Aquinas's metaphysical assumptions and derivations. If, for example, we don't buy into the concept of actuality and potentiality, or that perfection is explained in terms of actuality, along with several other assumptions, then the data we get from these derivations will be of little, if any, value.

Suppose we don't share these specific metaphysical assumptions of Aquinas, what then? All is likely not lost, since we might be able to make less metaphysical assumptions, or assumptions others will find more plausible, so as to acquire some data about the divine. For instance, if we take the divine to be the source of all contingent reality, we can say that the divine can't depend upon anything contingent for its existence and therefore must be distinct from contingent reality. What this actually entails will largely depend upon the metaphysical assumptions one adopts about what contingent reality is. For instance, if one takes the spatio-temporal world to be contingent, then the divine can't depend upon it and will therefore be distinct from the spatio-temporal world. One might be inclined to think that this would mean that the divine is non-temporal, but this would require us to endorse the metaphysical view that there is no time distinct from that which describes the spatio-temporal world, and this is something that some reject. The result is that it will be consistent to say that the divine is distinct from the spatio-temporal world whilst also saying that the divine is temporal, albeit temporal in a sense that isn't dependent on the contingent spatio-temporal world.[66]

However, we can conclude more about the divine from the fact that it is distinct from all contingent reality, for this would seem to imply that the divine cannot itself be contingent and must therefore be necessary. From this necessity, we might be able to deduce various other attributes the divine possesses. Avicenna, for example, attempted to do just this, arguing that from the divine's necessity one can conclude that there can only be one divine being and that the divine is simple (Zarepour, 2022). Once again, deductions such as these will often rely on metaphysical positions that some might find implausible, or may rely upon moves that one finds questionable, and therefore will only be compelling to those who think the presuppositions and deductions are plausible.

If we add into the mix additional assumptions, such as 'everything other than the divine' is co-extensive with 'all contingent reality', then we can also conclude from our starting point that the divine is unique (Kvanvig, 2021, 12). Moreover, in virtue of being the source of all contingent reality, we can say that the divine has power, since all contingent reality depends

---

[66] For example, this view is adopted by Padgett (1992).

upon it.⁶⁷ We might then attempt to combine this thought about power with the thought that the divine isn't spatio-temporal, and suggest that the only beings that have powers and are non-spatio-temporal are unembodied minds, and therefore conclude that the divine is an unembodied mind (Craig & Sinclair, 2009, 193).⁶⁸

It may well be that further deductions about the divine nature can be made in virtue of it being the source of all contingent reality, but what I've said here should provide us with some idea as to how to go about acquiring data about the divine via CT.⁶⁹ However, even though we're able to ascertain some data about the divine in this way, most acknowledge that we're still left with a 'gap problem', since these deductions alone aren't thought to give us a comprehensive understanding of the divine. This may be less concerning if we have multiple sources of data and can pool them together to create a comprehensive model of the divine. We might also think that this isn't a gap we should want to fill, for we're trying to gather data about the divine without presupposing what the divine is like, as we will then use this data to formulate a model of the divine. Nevertheless, people do think it's a problem that something like Law's (2010) 'evil-god' is consistent with the deductions we've made thus far via the non-Thomistic CT, since nothing about the divine's moral character has been deduced. Further, much of the data we've acquired says nothing as to whether the attributes in question, say power, are maximal, and so these deductions can also provide us with data for a being that possesses limited powers.⁷⁰ What some have therefore attempted to do is think about ways in which we can further fill out the data we've acquired from this methodology.

One way, proposed by Swinburne, suggests that in virtue of thinking about simplicity, we get some reason for thinking that the attributes of a divine being will be maximal. He does this by first suggesting that

---

⁶⁷ The dependence language here could be understood causally, but even if it were understood as a type of ontological dependence, this would still lead to most people thinking that the divine possessed power, since divine causation was historically understood more along the lines of contemporary notions of ontological dependence (Cohoe, 2013, 839, n.4).

⁶⁸ From the fact that the divine is an unembodied mind, some have attempted to derive that the divine must be a person. But personhood is sometimes derived in another way, namely by suggesting that the only type of explanation we can give for the existence of all contingent reality must be a personal explanation, and from this concluding that that which explains all contingent reality is personal (Swinburne, 2004, 133–152).

⁶⁹ For a good discussion of different ways that have been proposed to deduce attributes see Ocampo (2024) and Rasmussen (2010, 813–815).

⁷⁰ The data in question is consistent with the divine possessing maximal power or limited power, since it merely entails that the divine has *at least* some limited powers.

simpler theories are to be preferred on the grounds that they are more likely to be true (Swinburne, 1997), and then contends that it is simpler to assume that any attribute of the divine which is gradable is maximal since an infinite attribute is simpler than a finite one (Swinburne, 2004, 54–55; Miller, 2016). Here it seems we have a type of idealisation occurring, albeit one that is supposed to provide us a more accurate understanding of the divine given our finite intellectual capabilities. Therefore, if we agree with Swinburne and his presuppositions, we have a way of acquiring data which suggests that the divine possesses attributes of infinite nature, rather than merely finite ones.

However, Swinburne thinks that if we do have reason for positing 'pure, limitless, intentional power' (1994, 151) then we can deduce many other attributes of the divine. For instance, he suggests that we should think that the divine must be free, since nothing external could exert a causal influence over pure, limitless, intentional power (1994, 152) and that in virtue of having pure, limitless, intentional power the divine should be thought to be both omniscient (1994, 152–153) and to exist everlastingly (1994, 153). Elsewhere, Swinburne argues that so long as we think that the divine is a person and exists everlastingly, we can conclude that it is a perfectly free omniscient spirit which is perfectly good, the source of moral obligation, and the creator of any world there is (2016, 244).[71] Spelling out Swinburne's reasons for these deductions is beyond the scope of this Element, but it shows how some might attempt to use deductive means to spell out the nature of the divine further. *If* we can deduce all of what Swinburne suggests, then that's pretty impressive, but once again the question will be whether we find the deductions and assumptions required for them plausible, and that is for you, my reader, to ascertain.

Rasmussen (2020; 2024; Rasmussen & Leon, 2019, 112–115) also attempts to provide a reason for thinking that the attributes we can derive via CT are maximal. One way he does this is by suggesting that we should prefer that data that posits fewer arbitrary limits, especially when thinking about something foundational or divine. Thus, suppose we consider divine power. If we say that divine power is finite, someone might ask why it is limited to this particular finite extent rather than another. If there's no good answer to this question, then it seems we're left with an arbitrary limit on power. Supposing we have reason to prefer those theories that limit arbitrariness over those that don't, we can suggest that we've got reason for preferring a conception of divine power that is not limited, but limitless.

---

[71] See Swinburne (2016, chs. 7–12) for the justification.

We might think that this lack of arbitrariness would only help if we had reason to think that the postulation of maximal power itself weren't arbitrary, and here Rasmussen contends that it isn't arbitrary, since he thinks the least arbitrary foundation of reality would be one that would have no limits whatsoever and whose fundamental nature would imply that it has none of these limits. Here, the notion of perfection comes back into play, for Rasmussen proposes that 'A perfect thing … is precisely the sort of thing that would lack fundamental limits, boundaries, and arbitrary specificities' (2024, 328; 2020, 30; Rasmussen & Leon, 2019, 114–115). The result of this is that if we agree with Rasmussen's methodology, CT can lead into PBT, and PBT can become relevant even when using CT's way of acquiring data.

Employing reasoning about perfection also plays a role in other non-deductive ways of filling out the data we have ascertained via CT. For example, Byerly, when thinking about the attribute of necessary existence, suggests that the best answer to the question 'why does this being have this attribute?' is 'because it is a perfect being – a being possessing all perfections – and necessary existence is a perfection.' (2019, 12) Here an abductive inference is being made, namely moving from a being which has some of the perfections to a being which has all the perfections. Whilst Byerly's focus is on the conclusions of cosmological arguments, Mooney (2019) shows how the same type of move can be made when considering the conclusions of fine-tuning arguments. Miksa (2023) has also suggested that another type of abductive inference, this time based on aesthetic virtues, would lead us from the conclusion that the divine is the cause of all contingent reality to the claim that it is a PB. The result of all this is that if we find any of these inferences plausible, then we will be able to move from CT to PBT, which would enable us to deduce other attributes of the PB, and demonstrates that one does not have to see these methodologies as entirely separate.

Before concluding this section, let me draw attention to the fact that some of the ways of acquiring additional data about the divine have relied on what we might call 'theoretical virtues', with these virtues supposedly giving us reason to think that some type of data should be preferred or postulated.[72] Whilst these virtues may have more of a role to play when sorting our data, it is worth noting that this type of methodology, although

---

[72] Within the context of philosophy of religion, Oppy (2013; Oppy & Pearce, 2022) is a prime example of someone who suggests that we should judge theories on their theoretical virtues. It may well be that these theoretical virtues would play a role if we have to compare models of the divine too.

having many adherents in philosophy, also has many detractors. The reason for this is that there appears to be various questions theoretical virtues raise, for which we seem to struggle to provide good answers to. For instance, is there a set of virtues that we should privilege, and if so, what are these virtues? Supposing we could concoct such a list, how should we prioritise these virtues if and when they conflict with each other? There are other questions to ask here too, but unless philosophers can agree on how to answer them it seems there will likely be many irresolvable disagreements. Additionally, more needs to be done to show that these virtues guide one towards the truth, rather than provide merely aesthetic reasons (Maclaurin & Dyke, 2012, 304) for preferring one theory over another. This is even more the case since these virtues were not originally postulated for work done in metaphysics and theological construction, but rather science and philosophy of science, with some even suggesting that satisfying the theoretical virtues in the scientific domain does nothing to tell us the truth about the theory in question (van Frassen, 1985, 252). It may well be that there are good answers to these questions, but they will be the types of question one should consider if they wish to bring ideas of theological virtues into modelling the divine.

4.3 Worship-Worthiness and Holiness

Let me conclude this section by briefly talking about two other recent proposals that have been recommended for ascertaining data about the divine nature via reason. The first, proposed by Kvanvig (2021, 30), suggests that when we consider what the divine is like we should start with the thought that it is a being worthy of worship, or more precisely, that the divine is 'maximally worthy of the most supreme worship, and most distinctively so.' Much like the previous two approaches, the idea is that from this starting point we can then deduce various attributes which the divine must possess in order to be worthy of worship. For instance, Kvanvig thinks that because worship is 'a communicative act, and such communicative acts make sense only when directed at things with intelligence and will – which is to say, to persons' (2021, 112–113), we are given good reason to think that the divine is a person.

Whilst Kvanvig thinks that the divine being a person is required in order for worship of the divine to make sense, we might ask what it is that makes this being worthy of worship in the first place, or in other words, what grounds worship-worthiness? Asking this question might cause some to worry that if worship-worthiness is grounded, then worship-worthiness cannot be fundamental to the divine and so perhaps doesn't provide us with a good starting place to acquire data about the divine. In terms of fundamentality, it is true that a widespread thought is that if y grounds x, then y is more fundamental than x (e.g. Rosen, 2010, 116), and that something is fundamental if it is not grounded (e.g. Rosen, 2010, 113). If this is right, then if something grounds worship-worthiness, then worship-worthiness can't be a fundamental feature of the divine, since that which grounds worship-worthiness is more fundamental, perhaps even being ungrounded. One might reply by objecting to this criterion of fundamentality by claiming that there are fundamental entities where it is the case that x grounds y and y grounds x,[73] and so perhaps in our case worship-worthiness grounds some other attributes of the divine and these attributes ground worship-worthiness. However, Kvanvig doesn't take this route; rather he contends, following Williamson (2000), that at least one thing, knowledge, can be grounded by things like belief truth, and so forth, and yet knowledge is fundamental. As such, he thinks the same could be the case with worship-worthiness (2022, 31), being both grounded and fundamental.[74] But we might also question whether we require worship-worthiness to be fundamental in order to acquire data about the divine from it, for it seems that all we actually need is worship-worthiness to be an *essential* feature of the divine. If it is essential then the divine will always have this attribute, and as such we can ask both what grounds this feature and what we can derive about the divine in virtue of it having this feature, with the answers to these questions providing us with data about what the divine may be like.[75]

What then grounds worship-worthiness? Here, it's at least plausible to think that the answer will include being perfect (Kvanvig, 2021, 164–165), and as such worship-worthiness is at least partially grounded in the fact that the being in question is a PB. Yet going this route seems to once again lead into the methodology of PBT, since it is PBT which informs us as to exactly what these perfections are. However, one might reply that worship-worthiness isn't grounded in perfection; Nagasawa (2008, 595), for example, has suggested something like this. He asks us to consider a thought experiment where a certain being has all the traditional omni-attributes except omniscience, since the being in question lacks knowledge of one trivial truth. In virtue of this ignorance, we might think that the

---

[73] See Giannotti (2021, 578–579) for discussion.
[74] See Kvanvig (2021, 31–33) for more on grounding worship-worthiness.
[75] Perhaps, merely thinking of worship-worthiness as essential might lead to worship-worthiness being multiply realised, whereas if it is fundamental this wouldn't be the case. Whether this is problematic isn't something I can deal with here.

being in question cannot count as a PB, and as we'll see in Section 5.2, this is what advocates of what I'll call strong-PBT would contend, and therefore in virtue of failing to be perfect, it cannot be worship-worthy. Yet Nagasawa seems to think it strange to claim that if this being were to learn this trivial truth and become perfect it would then be worthy of worship, since he thinks that learning the trivial truth should have no impact as to whether the being is worship-worthy (2008, 595). There are at least two things that could be said in response here. The first is that someone who adopts a strong-PB account may claim that all the traditional omni-attributes are such that they come as a package deal rather than separately, and so the thought experiment on which this is based is an impossibility. The second is to contend that there is another form of PBT – which I'll call weak-PBT – that is not subject to the concern raised here, since weak-PBT doesn't require a PB to have all the omni-attributes (more on this in Section 5.2). As such, perfection could still be what grounds worship-worthiness, either partially or fully.

A final approach for providing a starting point to ascertain data about the divine has been proposed by Murphy (2021), who suggests that holiness is the appropriate starting point when thinking about the divine. Here the divine is said to be holy if it exhibits 'those features that make the dual *tremendum* and *fascinans* responses appropriate' (2021, 45); or in other words, 'the features that make the attraction to the holy one appropriate [*fascinans*] and the features that make it true that one would be out-of-place were the course of that attraction to be followed to completion [*tremendum*]' (2021, 45).[76] When considering *absolute* holiness, which Murphy takes to be what characterises the divine, 'it must be true that for all other subjects, union with that putatively holy being must be overwhelmingly attractive for those subjects ... and for any context of intimate relationship with the putatively holy one, there is a level of intimacy that is too close to be fitting for that being to occupy' (2021, 46–47). Supposing that we accept this characterisation, what data can we garner about the divine from this starting point? To answer this, we can ask, much as we had with worship-worthiness, what grounds holiness, since the grounds of holiness will supply us with some data regarding the divine nature.

The answer Murphy gives is that holiness is grounded in perfection, or more specifically, in strong-PBT. He writes, 'While we should say that the first-order features that make for divine perfection are metaphysically prior to God's holiness ... we can treat the affirmation of God's supreme

---

[76] For more on this understanding see Murphy (2021, ch. 2).

holiness as the, or an, evidential basis for affirming God's perfection' (2021, 57). Therefore, once again, we are led to consider the nature of perfection, and it is through conducting PBT that we can learn more about the divine. Nevertheless, Murphy still thinks the starting point of holiness is helpful, since it more easily allows us to infer that a priori-PBT ought to be undertaken on the basis of scripture. After all, scripture repeatedly calls the divine holy, and if understanding what it is to be holy requires that we conduct a priori-PBT to ascertain what grounds holiness, then the texts which speak of the divine being holy provide us with an indirect reason to conduct a priori-PBT (Murphy, 2021, 57–59).[77] Therefore, even with this methodology, we are drawn back into thinking about perfection in order to further apprehend what the divine is like.[78]

5 Data Sorting

Suppose that we've acquired data from all our various sources; now we must turn to the difficult business of sorting it into something less unruly so that it can be useful for informing our model of the divine. To do this I'll first focus on sorting the data that we have gathered from reason and then turn to sorting the data produced from all our different sources of acquisition. Let me give you fair warning though, that what you are about to read is quite abstract and theoretical in comparison to previous sections. However, as the author to the Hebrews states, 'Do not throw away your confidence; it will be richly rewarded' (10:35 NIV) – in Section 6, I will provide an example which will translate much of this abstract material into something more concrete. I therefore implore you, as you read this current section, to follow the command we are told God gave to Joshua: 'Be strong and brave. Do not be afraid. Do not lose hope' (Joshua 1:9 NIRV).

5.1 Sorting Reason's Data

As was evident in Section 4, there are several ways we may be able to gather data about the divine via reason. It might be, however, that one thinks only some ways of gathering data are epistemically valuable, since they find some methods, say via PBT, to be objectionable for various reasons. As such, suppose we have reason for thinking that only CT provides

---

[77] Note that this way of using scripture is different from Leftow's scriptural-PBT, since on Murphy's view scripture *does not* guide us as to what the perfections of the divine are. Rather, they just imply that a priori-PBT should be undertaken (2021, 58).

[78] Murphy (2021, 56–57) also suggests how holiness, perfection, and worship-worthiness are related to each other such that we might come to think of them not as wholly distinct but intimately related with each other.

epistemically valuable data, still there is work to be done, since we will want to ascertain if some of CT's data should be prioritised over other bits. Matters would be simpler if we thought that CT only provided us with one starting point for deducing other attributes about the divine (e.g. as 'a necessary being'). If this were the case, and suppose that we could directly deduce both p and q from this starting point, then I take it that both pieces of data should be weighed equally, unless one piece requires an assumption for its deduction that is more controversial than the other. What about if from p, one can deduce r, and from r, s? Should s be given equal weight to p? Here I'm inclined to think not, for the more deductions we make, the more chance we have of making an unintentional error, and/or assuming a questionable premise upon which our deduction relies. So if we were to consider data from one of our other sources of data acquisition, and found that this other data (which we took to be reliable) spoke against s or spoke against p, then I think we should more easily give up s as opposed to p.[79] This line of reasoning also seems to apply to the thoughts Swinburne and Rasmussen offered when suggesting how to increase the amount of data CT provides us with (i.e. by adopting some ideas regarding simplicity and/or no-arbitrary limits). So suppose that CT tells us that the divine has power, this data seems stronger than the data for thinking that the divine has infinite or unlimited power. For the data about the divine having power doesn't rely on the extra assumptions that Swinburne and Rasmussen require in order to conclude that the divine has infinite or unlimited power. However, if we were to think that we had just as good a reason for affirming the assumptions regarding simplicity and lacking arbitrary limits as we did for thinking the divine is 'a necessary being', then that the divine has infinite power will be just as well confirmed as the divine having power.[80]

But perhaps we think that CT can provide us with multiple distinct starting points, such as 'a necessary being' and 'a cause of finite temporal reality', and that these starting points can both offer data about the divine. How would this affect our ordering of the data? If the grounds for both of these starting points are equally plausible then it seems that the data we directly deduce from each of them will be as plausible as each other. But what if we can deduce p from both starting points, and only deduce

---

[79] We might ultimately conclude something more radical, perhaps that we should give up p too, or even that CT cannot be thought to provide reliable data.

[80] Suppose we rely upon theoretical virtues either in our data acquisition or data sorting and these conflict, then it will be up to us to make a judgement about which virtue we should prefer so we can order the data accordingly.

Modelling the Divine

q from one starting point? Here it seems we should weigh p more heavily than q. This might lead us to think that if something about the divine can be deduced from both starting points it should always be weighed more heavily than if it could only be deduced from one. But it's not obvious that this is always the case. To see this, suppose that from 'a necessary being' we can deduce x; and from x, y; and from y, z. Meanwhile, from 'a cause of finite temporal reality' we can deduce q; and from q, z. What should we think of z's epistemic value? If x and y are consistent with 'a cause of finite temporal reality' and q is consistent with 'a necessary being', then it seems we should say that z is more epistemically valuable than if it was merely deduced from only one starting point.[81] What about if x were inconsistent with 'a cause of finite reality' and q were inconsistent with a necessary being? Here it doesn't seem that we should conclude that z is more epistemically valuable in virtue of being derived from two different starting points, since the way it is derived means that given one's starting point, there will only be one consistent way in which it can be derived.

What about if there were incompatibilities from only one starting point, say with x being inconsistent with 'a cause of finite reality'? Given that we're taking both starting points as having equal epistemic value, we might think z is just as epistemically valuable as in the previous case. But if we think one starting point has more epistemic value than the other, then it may make a difference. So if we thought 'a cause of finite reality' should be prioritised, then z would have the epistemic value of being derivable from one source. But if we prioritised 'a necessary being' (since this starting point is consistent with the way 'a cause of finite reality' deduces z), then it would seem z has more epistemic value, since it accrues this value in virtue of being deducible from two starting points. In addition to this, how much weight we give z overall (relative to other attributes we can deduce from two starting points) likewise depends upon how many derivations it takes to arrive at the attribute in question, since attributes which require fewer derivations should be considered more epistemically valuable than those which require more, as they leave less room for questionable assumptions or errors to occur.

What are we to do, then, in a case where direct derivations from the two different starting points are incompatible? If we didn't weigh both starting points equally, then we would have reason to prefer the data accrued

---

[81] Given what I said above, since there are fewer deductions required to get to z from 'a cause of finite reality' compared with 'a necessary being', we can think z individually accrues more epistemic value as a data point from 'a cause of finite reality' when compared with 'a necessary being'.

from the starting point we take to be more plausible, since this data, all else being equal, would always be prioritised over that which was derived from the other starting point. But as we are taking both starting points to be of equal value then the best option seems to be to appeal to other data that we acquire from other sources in order to see if this helps us ascertain which data should be prioritised.

So far we've been supposing that only one method of data acquisition via reason is epistemically valuable, but one might equally think all the ways we've discussed of acquiring data via reason are acceptable. If we do then we'll need to answer the additional question as to whether we think all these methods provide data of equal epistemic value. For instance, we might think that the data PBT produces has *some* epistemic value, but less than that gathered by CT. If we were to think this, then we would always prefer the data gathered by CT, prioritising it over that produced by PBT. PBT's data may, however, still be useful, since it could help to resolve any incompatibilities in the data CT produces, or provide us with more information about the divine (so long as what it says is consistent with data from CT). Alternatively, we might think that the data CT and PBT yield are equal in epistemic value, and therefore neither should be prioritised. Suppose for the sake of simplicity we think this, we then need to ask what this implies for our data sorting. However, before answering this question, it will first be helpful to sort the data we have acquired through PBT, and we can do this by turning to the second stage of PBT.

5.2 PBT Stage Two – Sorting Potential Perfections

After stage one of PBT what we've acquired is a list of those attributes that we take to be *pure* perfections, be this via a priori-PBT or scriptural-PBT, along with any derivations we can make from these pure perfections. If all of these perfections and derivations are compatible, then according to PBT the divine has them all and the job of PBT is over, having provided us with data that either fully, or partially, describes the divine's intrinsic nature.

Yet happy endings are sadly not always possible and so suppose that after sorting out which pure perfections are consistent, we are left with others that are seemingly incompatible. What are we to do?[82]

Here it's helpful to make a distinction between strong-PBT and weak-PBT, since which position we take will determine what we do next. On strong-PBT the divine 'exhibits absolute, unlimited, unmottled perfection'

---

[82] Even Anselm was aware that PBT might lead to one thinking there are incompatible perfections. Some of these are discussed in his *Proslogion*.

(Murphy, 2021, 57). By contrast, on weak-PBT the divine has the best possible consistent set of perfections.[83] To characterise this another way, on weak-PBT trade-offs between perfections may be required, on strong-PBT, by contrast, there are no trade-offs. So whereas a weak-PB might have maximal goodness and less than maximal power, so to avoid any supposed incompatibility between the two, and yet still be considered a PB, a strong-PBT theorist will not allow such a weakening of the attributes. As Murphy, an advocate of strong-PBT notes,

> one cannot simply truncate a perfection by characterizing it in a way that it does not generate conflict; one must do so in a way that explains *why* the truncation does not involve yielding any value but is only a clarification of how a being might reach maximal metaphysically possible greatness along that dimension. For example, on the traditional view, it is perfectly fine to say that the fact that God does not exhibit a level of power that is intrinsically impossible to realize does not count as making God less than perfect; it is not fine to say that God exhibits less than maximal power simply in order to make sure that it fits with other divine perfections. … It must be impossible for the absolutely perfect being to be worse than any other being along *any* dimension of perfection.[84] (Murphy, 2017, 11; italics original)

The result of this is that strong-PBT will lead us to a PB which has the omni-attributes, whereas weak-PBT won't imply that a PB has omni-attributes, with this fact having implications for the last two views I talked about in Section 4.3, namely conceptions of the divine which start from worship-worthiness or holiness.[85] For instance, the argument Nagasawa gave about perfection not being able to ground worship-worthiness, which I mentioned previously, presupposes that a PB must be a strong-PB, but if one disagrees and thinks that a PB is in fact a weak-PB, then arguably Nagasawa's concern about worship-worthiness can be overcome, since it can no longer rely on the strong-PB presupposition

---

[83] For a defender of weak-PBT see Nagasawa (2017). Murphy sometimes calls this view 'revisionist' PBT, and provides some critical discussion of it (2017, 10–19; 2021, ch. 3).

[84] This final claim holds what we might call the *distributive assumption*, where 'God exhibits the maximal level of the divine perfections, understood distributively – for *each* unqualified good-making property that God exhibits, God exhibits *that property* to the intrinsic maximum of its value' (Murphy, 2017, 12). This contrasts a different assumption about the perfections, what we might call the *atomist assumption*, which holds that 'for each perfection, what constitutes the intrinsic maximum of the value of that perfection is independent of that perfection's relation to other divine perfections' (Murphy, 2017, 12). Which assumption a PBT theorist should run with is something they'll need to consider too.

[85] Note that the claim that PBT delivers the omni-attributes is sometimes employed in arguing against PBT (Nagasawa, 2017, 90–94), but ultimately it should only be understood as arguing against strong-PBT.

(Kvanvig, 2021, 166–167). By contrast, Murphy contends that absolute holiness is incompatible with a weak-PB, since he thinks that adopting this view will allow there to always be contexts in which the divine does not meet the conditions of absolute holiness (2021, 47–53), and therefore absolute holiness will require a strong-PB.

Suppose that we were to adopt strong-PBT, what are we to do in light of supposed incompatibilities between the *pure* perfections? The first thing we could do is suggest that we haven't properly explained what the attributes in question amount to and that we might have mischaracterised them in some way, with this being why we have a *seeming* incompatibility. For Murphy, characterising the perfections in such a way as 'to secure both the internal consistency of the alleged perfection and the coherence of that alleged perfection with other affirmed perfections' (2017, 11) is what he takes to be the second stage of strong-PBT.[86] Suppose, however, we try to fail in achieving this. Then there will be two options left to us. The first is to reconsider whether the perfection in question really is a pure perfection, since if we come to think that it's not pure, it will no longer be an incompatibility we must resolve, since we're only considering the divine to have all pure perfections. Alternatively, we will have to appeal to mystery and claim that these *pure* perfections are in fact consistent, but just in a way that is *presently* mysterious to us.[87] Once we've made our choice and taken the relevant steps, we will be left with a strong-PB which has a consistent set of attributes, with all of the gradable attributes that it possesses being at their maximum value. If we can make any derivations from this, then these pure perfections, along with any derivations, will be the data that strong-PBT provides.

By contrast, if we adopt weak-PBT, the data we will end up with will be the best possible or best conceivable set of attributes, and so the process we undertake when dealing with potential incompatibilities between pure perfections will be different. To start, we will group the pure perfections into compatible sets and then see if any pure perfections are present across all sets. If there are any, then a weak-PB has these perfections. Next, we can attempt what strong-PBT suggests, and see if we have made a mistake

---

[86] This does not mean one can come up with ad hoc descriptions of the attributes to avoid incompatibilities, for as Murphy says, 'One has to show that the property so characterized can not only be coherently ascribed to a being along with the other divine perfections; it must also be shown that the property so characterized is at the intrinsic maximum of value for exhibiting that feature' (2017, 11).

[87] However, when it comes to seemingly straightforward contradictions, appealing to mystery doesn't seem like a plausible response (Pawl, 2016, 88–91).

in the way in which we explain any of the perfections so as to avoid some of these incompatibilities, and if we do so in such a way that more pure perfections are had across all sets, then we can also add these into the pile of perfections that a weak-PB has. But suppose not all incompatibilities are resolved in this way and we don't see any good reason to reconsider whether the perfections in question are pure. At such a juncture, we must enter the realm of trade-offs.

Here we must consider whether we have reason to think that some of the pure perfections are more valuable than others, since if some are more valuable, these will be prioritised when an incompatibility occurs, providing us with some reason to weaken those attributes which are considered less valuable.[88] To do this, it's clear that a judgement about value will need to be made by the advocate of weak-PBT, and since these judgements can vary amongst theorists, this may lead to different characterisations as to what a weak-PB is. So, to take one example, Leftow, when conducting PBT, thinks that love should be prioritised (2018a, 106–109), whilst Murphy, albeit an advocate of strong-PBT, doesn't think this (2017, 22–44; 2021, 98–108).[89] Once an advocate of weak-PBT has made these judgments they can once again look across their set of attributes, with some now being weakened, and see if there are any new attributes that are shared across all the sets. If there are, then these too will be added to the pot of attributes that a weak-PB possesses.

But what if there are still incompatibilities left amongst the attributes that we take to be of equal or incommensurable value, then here, as Leftow says, 'One has to ask what each "costs." That is, one must ask what something "loses" if it gets F and not G, or G and not F. The perfect being theologian then picks the lower-cost attribute' (2022a, 291). If we can work out that some pure perfections cost more than others, then we should pick the lower cost perfections to weaken. Then, once again, if after having done this we find new commonalities across our sets of attributes, then these will also get into our package of describing a weak-PB. However, if we are still left with some incompatibilities, then at this point

---

[88] This relates to what De Haan (2023, 101) calls the 'ordering-attributes problem', which asks which divine attributes are given priority over others and why. I suspect he wouldn't be impressed by the claim that this requires a judgement by the person conducting weak-PBT.

[89] Ultimately this is because Murphy thinks there isn't a pure perfection regarding love, even though he still wants to say the divine is loving (2021, 98). But one could imagine a debate occurring where one thought love was a *pure* perfection but that it wasn't a *pure* perfection which should be prioritised over some other *pure* perfections due to some of the reasons Murphy gives.

we should say that a weak-PB possesses the disjunction of these incompatible attributes.[90] After this process, and after any further deductions we can make, we will have ended up with a single description of a weak-PB and the job of weak-PBT is over.[91]

5.3 Finishing Sorting Reason's Data

Now that we've sorted the data that strong and weak-PBT can give us, we can think about its relationship to CT, where we recall that we are assuming that both PBT and CT give us data of the same epistemic value. Suppose then that both acquisition methods give us independent reason to affirm a particular attribute, then I suggest that this means we should think such data has more epistemic value compared with data that is given by only one method. If, by contrast, PBT and CT provide us with incompatible attributes, then we should think that these bits of data are less epistemically valuable than data which is supported by only one of the acquisition methods but is compatible with the data produced by the other. Additionally, given that we are taking the data of CT to be of the same weight as that of PBT, we might employ the data of CT when thinking about stage two of PBT. For instance, when dealing with incompatibilities, it might help inform us as to whether a perfection should be thought of as a pure perfection or not, for perhaps if one perfection is also posited by CT whilst another is not, we might have more reason to reassess the non-shared perfection than the shared one. Equally, it might help us in determining which perfections should be adjusted in any trade-offs we make, with those perfections that are also postulated by CT being ones that we should seek not to trade-off in the first instance. Furthermore, even if after employing the data of both methods we arrive at the same types of incompatibilities that we arrived at when employing only one, this might give us an additional reason to play the 'mystery card' compared with when just one of the data methods resulted in this incompatibility. However, it may be that we can avoid this type of move once we incorporate all the data from our other sources, since doing so might show us what is to be prioritised when considering incompatibilities. Given that we

---

[90] In other words, we should say that a weak-PB possesses either j or k, where j and k are incompatible attributes.

[91] This isn't to say that this is all one could discuss regarding PBT as a whole, since there is *much* more. See for instance Nagasawa (2017), Mawson (2019), Rogers (2000), Murphy (2017, ch. 1), and Leftow (forthcoming a). For some critical analysis of PBT see Kvanvig (2021) and, in particular, Speaks (2018), with Leftow providing multiple replies to Speaks's arguments (2022b; 2023; 2024; in press).

Modelling the Divine 43

have by and large sorted out all the data that reason can provide us with, we can now turn to thinking about how it interacts with data accrued from other sources.

5.4 Sorting *All* of Our Data

When we come to sorting out all of our data, we will need to ask similar questions to the ones we've just considered when we thought about sorting the data produced by reason. Once again, we can start by asking whether we should prioritise data acquired from some methods over data gathered from others. Should the data garnered from scripture be considered more valuable than the data from experience, or does one's reason offer better quality data than data that is received from traditions? Here it may also be appropriate to ask more fine-grained questions, like whether a specific piece of data from a source is more valuable than another specific piece of data from another source (since, for example, it might be that we think *some* traditions are more valuable than reason, but not *all* traditions).

Answering these types of questions is a difficult task, and it may well be that our answers will depend upon whether one belongs to a particular religious tradition and the content of one's background knowledge and assumptions. However, if it were to turn out that the data from all the different collection methods was consistent, then answering which, if any, acquisition method should be thought of as giving us data to be preferred might not need answering. However, thinking that this will occur is rather optimistic, and it seems very likely that there will be inconsistencies amongst our data sets. What are we to do in this case?

Before suggesting how we might approach this, it might be helpful to sort all our data out more generally. To do this, we can start by grouping the data into categories where there is agreement amongst the acquisition methods. If we do this, and if there is some data which is found across all our data collection methods, then this is the data about the divine we should take to be most trustworthy. We can continue grouping the data in a similar way, such that we have sets where the data is collected by three different methods, and then two, and finally one.[92] Here, supposing we accept at present the simplifying assumption that all the data acquisition

---

[92] The sets here could be more specific, such that we group our data according to which sources produce this data, and therefore since we have four general methods of data acquisition, we will have four different groupings of three data acquisition methods, and six different groupings of two acquisition methods. This way of ordering things would be especially helpful if we ended up ranking the value of each data acquisition method differently.

methods produce data of equal epistemic value, then we should think that the data that can be retrieved via three methods is superior to the data collected via one or two.

If we assume this to be the case, we can then look at the data in each set to see if we can order how epistemically valuable it is in relation to the set, since it might be that some of the data in each of these groupings is more valuable than others. To see this, note that a data acquisition method might produce the same data either once or repeatedly. For instance, as I've suggested above, reason might produce the same data point in various ways. So too might scripture repeatedly speak about a particular piece of data, and we may therefore think that the data which is spoken of frequently is of more epistemic value than that which is spoken of rarely, with the same being said for both tradition and experience.[93] The reason we might say it is of greater epistemic value is that we might consider data acquired more frequently to be more reliable (since such data is regularly attested to). Supposing we agree with this, then we can order the data in our groupings in terms of frequency, and at the end of this process, we will have different piles of data that are sorted in terms of the data collection methods that produce this data, as well as how frequently the data is produced by these methods. With this sorting done, we can claim that the most epistemically valuable data will be that which is found in all the methods with the greatest frequency, and the least valuable will be that which is found in only one of the methods and with the least frequency.

How then should we address any incompatibilities between our bits of data assuming all the acquisition methods are of equal value? Depending upon where the incompatibility is to be found, this may be more or less easy to say. For suppose there is an incompatibility between a piece of data that is found in all our methods of acquisition and at the greatest frequency, and a piece of data that is found in only one data acquisition method and only once. In this case it seems that after failing to make them compatible, we should drop the least well attested piece of data in favour of the most well attested. But what are we to do if, by chance, the incompatible data concerns two pieces which are found in all data acquisition methods and attested to most frequently? Here we have a few different options. First, we might see if there is any way to reinterpret the data so as to make it consistent. If this fails, then we might start with both bits

---

[93] As I said earlier, if one holds to a dictation view of scripture, then the fact that something is spoken of multiple times in scripture compared with only once doesn't seem to have any bearing on its epistemic trustworthiness.

of incompatible data and see what other bits of data they are compatible with. For if it turns out that one of the bits of data is incompatible with most of the other data we have acquired, whilst the other is compatible with vast swathes of the data we have collected, then we should likely prefer the piece of data which is compatible with most of the other data we have collected. But how about if we end up in a situation where roughly the same amount of data is compatible with both bits of data? Here, something I've yet to talk about explicitly may come into play, namely our prior commitments.

5.5 Prior Commitments

When we're thinking about prioritising data and generating a model, it may be that we have prior commitments that would lead us to prefer a certain piece of data over another. To give an example, suppose there are some metaphysical theses that we hold independently of anything to do with theorising about the divine, and which we take to be well confirmed. Given this, any piece of data about the divine which clashes with this confirmed prior commitment may be questioned in virtue of this clash. This might be helpful when we are dealing with data about the divine which is incompatible, as we can also ask how this data relates to our prior commitments, since if one piece of data clashes with these commitments whilst the other doesn't, we ought to drop the data which clashes and endorse the data that doesn't.

However, there is another question we need to consider here, namely when we should allow the data to change our prior commitments. Supposing that most of the data we possess about the divine clashes with some prior commitment we hold, then it might be that what we ought to do is reject this prior commitment instead of all the data that it clashes with. Exactly when we should take this posture is difficult to say, but it certainly doesn't seem like it should be something that is ruled out from the get-go.

Note also that one's prior commitments are likely to affect both the data we possess and derivations we make based on this data. For instance, if we adopt Aquinas's metaphysical framework as a prior commitment, then his style of CT will look very attractive to us, as will the derivations about the divine that he makes. But if we don't adopt these prior metaphysical commitments, instead preferring some other radically different metaphysical outlook, then his way of doing things likely won't be at all attractive. To take another example, we've seen different people come to diverse conclusions about what counts as a perfection when conducting PBT, but the reason for this is likely based on people adopting different prior commitments as to what is valuable.[94] The derivations people find plausible will also likely be somewhat determined by their prior commitments, for if someone thinks that something other than an immaterial mind can be both immaterial and have causal power, they won't be persuaded by those derivations which rely on the thought that only a mind can be both immaterial and have power. Finally, what one prioritises in one's data and how one thinks the data should be explained may also be dependent upon one's prior commitments. This can be seen from O'Connor and Montgomery's review of Sider's *Writing the Book of the World* (2011), where they conclude that Sider, and those 'contemporary metaphysicians embracing this sort of radical reductionism ... need to get out more' (2013). But the reason they conclude this is largely that they possess different prior commitments to Sider and those who embrace this 'austere vision of reality' (O'Connor & Montgomery, 2013). Therefore, even though they are all attempting to explain the general features of our world, the data they prioritise is different and how they go about explaining this data is different too.

Therefore, since each person possesses different prior commitments that may play a role in formulating their model of the divine as well providing them with reason to prioritise different bits of data, it is useful to be as upfront about these as possible, since it will make it more transparent where our prior commitments may affect an outcome. For the reality is that two different theorists could by and large agree on what the data is but still produce substantially different models of the divine due to having different prior commitments.

5.6 Back to Sorting

Turning back to the example we were considering before our detour, suppose that even after thinking about our prior commitments we are in the unfortunate position of having incompatibilities between epistemologically significant pieces of data. What are we to do then? Perhaps something more radical will be required.

One thing that we could do would be to question a prior commitment that I've so far assumed, namely that we want our data to be consistent. The reason for this is that contradictions are typically taken as being a bad

---

[94] For instance, some have gone so far to assert that the conclusions of PBT are actually distinctively Western, white, and masculine, implying that people from more marginalised communities would provide an alternative list of perfections (for references, see Wood, 2021, 261). This may constitute an objection to PBT, although assessing whether it is a good one will have to wait for another occasion.

thing, even when we are considering the divine (Pawl, 2016, 88–91). But perhaps, if our data was overwhelmingly incompatible, this is something we should reconsider and maybe the most rational thing to do would be to give up on consistency. If we were to choose this type of option, then we might think that some contradictions to do with the divine are acceptable and that we therefore shouldn't be all that concerned about inconsistent data.[95]

Alternatively, perhaps we would draw a different conclusion from radical inconsistencies in the data we possess, namely in thinking that the divine is so utterly mysterious to us that we cannot speak of it consistently, and that to attempt to provide a model of it is a worthless pursuit. It is not that the divine itself *is* contradictory, but rather that we finite beings cannot comprehend the divine in a consistent manner given the data we possess about its nature.

A less radical option would be to suggest that we follow in the footsteps of weak-PBT and claim that for the data points that are inconsistent, our model of the divine just provides a disjunctive description of what the divine is like. This is obviously less than ideal, but models themselves are never ideal and are always limited, so perhaps this is the best we can hope to achieve in such cases. After all, why think we could do any better, especially when considering data from numerous sources about a divine being?

However, it may be that by removing the simplifying assumption of treating all our sources of data as providing data that of equal epistemic use, we can avoid various incompatibilities. For suppose one has reason to prioritise the data given to us from scripture over all other sources of data, then when a piece of data from experience clashes with data from scripture we will prioritise the data from scripture. Arguably, things will likely be more complicated in practice, since it might be that a given data point from experience is produced multiple times and supported by both reason and tradition, whilst the incompatible data point from scripture only comes from one obscure verse. In such an instance it may therefore be more rational to prioritise the data from experience instead. Yet if we have a sufficient reason to *always* prioritise the data of scripture, then perhaps the only use of data from experience will be to act as a tiebreaker if there is any inconsistency in the data of scripture, or in supplying other data which

---

[95] Even if inconsistencies in our data and model are allowed, this needn't imply that the model is incoherent, since arguably dialetheists have shown 'as clearly as anything like this can be shown, that it is coherent to maintain that some sentence can be both true and false at the same time.' (Parsons, 1990, 335). For an example of someone who adopts a view like this on a theological level see Beall (2021; 2023).

is consistent with what scripture claims. Whatever one does, the modeller will have to make a judgement as to how the data is to be weighed and how reliable we should think the sources of data acquisition are.

Obviously, if one chooses to prioritise data produced by one acquisition method over all others, then it would be helpful for the modeller to provide some reason for doing this. One reason we might prefer the data of some sources is that we think these sources can better answer the questions we raised of them in Section 3 on data acquisition, when compared with others. Nonetheless, because one cannot hope to achieve everything in a philosophical discussion, one might think that in the process of providing a model of the divine we don't need to provide reasons as to why we prefer some sources of data compared with others, but rather we can just state that this judgement is an assumption that we will take for granted, perhaps providing an additional promissory note that this is something we can back up at a future time if needed.

Additionally, it's important to see that if we prioritise one data source over others, then this may affect the data that we collect from these other methods of acquisition in various ways. For instance, suppose that we prioritise tradition, and tradition informs us how to think of perfection or how to interpret scripture. Then the conclusions we reach via PBT and the data we extract from scripture may be very different than if we hadn't prioritised tradition and merely relied on our own intuitions as to what perfection is and what scripture claims. This isn't to suggest that doing this is problematic, but once again, it is helpful to acknowledge, especially since it may show how two people can seem to have all the same data and yet still produce wildly different models of the divine.

Given all of this discussion, what should be clear is that sorting our data is a very difficult task and requires us to think about many different things and make numerous judgements. However, supposing that we have sorted our data, then we will be able to identify the data which we think most accurately portrays the divine nature. From this, we might see if we can make any further derivations, to see if there is more we can say about the divine, but once this is done we will be left with our model of the divine.

Since it is impractical to think that when we are going through the process of data acquisition and sorting we will have gathered and considered all possible data and be aware of all the presuppositions which may affect our outcome, we may still say that our model is not fully informed. But it's likely that we'll never be able to produce such a model, and that the best we can hope for is a well-informed model of the divine, where this still will require a decent amount of data and analysis of what we are doing in order to produce something useful. Exactly what counts as 'decent' will again be difficult to determine, but models which adequately consider more relevant data should, all else being equal, be preferred over those which consider less. Yet the nice thing about modelling is that we can always incorporate more data to inform our model, and then, if necessary, adapt our model accordingly so as to account for this data.

Before moving on, let me conclude this section by noting that in the process of sorting there are likely to be some places where significant decision points will have to be made, with the route one chooses likely affecting much of what follows. Unfortunately, it's beyond the scope of this Element to talk about this in any detail here, but questions relating to whether the divine is a person will likely play a substantial role in determining what sort of model is produced, as will questions to do with whether the divine is simple and how simplicity should be understood.[96] Equally, considerations as to whether we should think there is one divine being or multiple, and whether its power should be prioritised over all else, will also shape, to a significant extent, the model we produce. The decisions we make regarding these and other topics can have important knock-on effects as to what the divine is like and how we think about the data we have accrued, and therefore they are decisions that we will need to spend additional time considering.

6 A Model Example

Now that we've finished discussing a modelling framework we can use when thinking about producing a model of the divine, it's time to get modelling! The aim of this section is therefore to provide a *very brief* run-through as to how we might put this framework to work in modelling a particular aspect of the divine. Since we will only be focusing on one aspect of the divine, we can consider this a 'toy model' which considers the divine's relationship to time. In order to simplify this process even further,

---

[96] How much questions of personhood affect things may in some cases be overblown (Page, 2019; Wood, 2021, ch. 9), compared with how discussions of so-called 'classical theism' and 'theistic personalism' see the issue. But there are other conceptions of the divine that are more obviously non-personal (Bishop & Perszyk, 2023; Gasser & Kittle, 2022). Note also that whilst so-called 'classical theism' and 'theistic personalism' might be somewhat helpful in teaching contexts, such groupings can often be unhelpful since they may lead one to think that all thinkers within these groups think about the divine in exactly the same way, both in terms of how to understand various attributes and their implications as well as related metaphysical issues, for which they surely don't. As the saying goes, 'the devil's in the details', and it is more useful to sketch the view out fully rather than relying on a general label that can be used to describe multiple views.

I'm going to assume that there are only two options before us regarding the divine's relationship to time, namely being temporal or timeless, where something is temporal if it exists at a time, and timeless if it exists at no time.[97] I'll also assume that our model should be consistent, and therefore the divine cannot be both temporal and timeless.

6.1 Data Acquisition

The first job is to collect some data in order to inform our model. I'm going to assume that we can collect data from all the sources I mentioned earlier in Section 3, but if you have a prior reason for thinking that one or more of the methods of data acquisition is a non-starter, then when you model you can ignore it as a data-gathering source. When acquiring data we can make another distinction that I've yet to talk about, namely data which is *directly* relevant to our question (whether the divine is temporal or timeless) and data that is *indirectly* relevant. Here directly relevant data is that data that doesn't require any intermediate steps for it to be relevant to what we are considering, whilst something is indirectly relevant if it requires some intermediate steps in order for it to be relevant.

6.1.1 Scripture

Suppose, to simplify matters once again, we limit ourselves to the Bible and assume that the text is inspired and that we are, by some means, able to gain propositional content about the divine from the text. Now we can ask whether it has any data that is directly relevant to whether the divine is temporal or timeless. It's far from clear to me that we do have any such data, as it's doubtful that the Bible anywhere speaks directly of the divine being temporal or timeless.[98] In contrast, if we were to ask whether the Bible gives us any direct data about divine knowledge the answer might be yes, with Job 37:16, for example, speaking of the divine as having 'perfect knowledge'.[99]

---

[97] Arguably there are other intermediate positions as well. See Leftow (2005b) and Craig (2001).

[98] Suppose we happened to think that the biblical authors speak as though the divine is temporal, with this judged to be an unthinking presumption or because speaking about the divine in an accessible way meant that the language used would imply temporality. Here we would need to make a judgment as to how much weight we should give to these texts in supporting divine temporality, and it may be that the right conclusion is that they provide little support. However, much more hermeneutical work would be needed to make a considered judgement here.

[99] Although it might not, given the genre, context, and vocabulary involved here.

However, the Bible does seem to provide lots of data that is indirectly relevant as to whether the divine is temporal or timeless. For this to be the case, there need to be things in the biblical text that imply, through some intermediate steps, that the divine is temporal or timeless. For example, we might think that if the divine changes then the divine is temporal, since timeless things cannot change. Therefore, any time the Bible speaks of the divine changing (e.g. Exodus 32:14) this implies that the divine is temporal. By contrast, if the Bible suggests that the divine doesn't change (e.g. Malachi 3:6), then this may suggest that the divine is in fact timeless rather than temporal, so long as temporal things do change.[100] Other indirect data may speak to our question too. For instance, supposing a timeless being cannot be a person, any time the Bible implies that the divine is a person we have data in favour of the divine being temporal. Or supposing that the divine is the source of all contingent reality and time is a contingent reality, when the Bible speaks of the divine being the source of all contingent reality, it speaks in favour of the divine being timeless. If a timeless being cannot bring the world into existence *ex nihilo* or act within time, then any time the Bible speaks of the divine doing this, it speaks in favour of temporality. Finally, suppose that the divine can only know the future free actions of creatures if it is timeless. Any time that the Bible speaks of the divine being able to do this, it provides us with reason for affirming timelessness. Whilst there is no doubt more Biblical data that is indirectly relevant to our question, this should give us an idea about the type of data one can accrue from the Bible.

6.1.2 Tradition

Here it's clear that the Christian tradition, at least, directly speaks of the divine as eternal, with eternity standardly being understood as speaking of 'timelessness' rather than 'temporally everlasting'.[101] Even those who think the divine is temporal, such as Hasker, admit as much, noting that thinking of the divine as timeless 'has been dominant historically' (Hasker, 2010, 81). Arguably, there is also some indirect support from tradition for the divine being timeless too, since tradition also suggests that the divine is simple (Dolezal, 2011, 3–10), and simplicity arguably entails timelessness (Leftow, 1991, 150–157).

---

[100] It would be important to look at the context of these verses to ascertain if they really are relevant to the question under consideration. Arguably Malachi 3:6 is not, but I use it here merely as an example.

[101] See Crisp (2019, 102–103) for some examples.

6.1.3 Experience

Experience doesn't seem to provide us with any direct data regarding the divine's relationship to time, but it may provide us with indirect data if we think that an experience of the divine requires that the divine interacts in time and that only temporal beings can act in time.[102] We might also think that experiences of the divine sometimes portray the divine as changing in some way, with this possibly giving us more indirect data for thinking that the divine is temporal.

6.1.4 Reason

CT might give us some reason for thinking that the divine is timeless, for supposing that CT implies that the divine creates all of contingent reality, then if time is a contingent reality, the divine would have created it. But if the divine has created time, then it must be able to exist without time, and as such the divine is timeless. There might be other starting points provided by CT that also point to the divine being temporal or timeless, but for simplicity we'll just stick with this one.

When thinking about PBT, we need to consider whether being temporal or timeless is a pure perfection. Prima facie one might think it's unclear that either are pure perfections. For instance, if timelessness brings with it the inability to act in time, then surely that is an imperfection. Likewise, if temporality implies that the divine is dependent on something distinct from itself, namely time, then this too might be thought an imperfection. Perhaps we should think the pure perfection PBT can arrive at is something like 'having the attribute of neither beginning nor ending'. Arguably both views of the divine's relationship to time wish to claim this, but how they go about doing so depends upon how we understand what it is for something to begin. For instance, supposing we understand a beginning as requiring that something was not and then is, then divine temporality, understood as temporally everlasting, won't imply that the divine begins or ends, and neither will timelessness, since something timeless cannot be said to begin or end.[103]

---

[102] I say 'seem' here, since in principle one could have a direct experience of the divine where the divine gives us direct data concerning the question we are considering, by saying to us, 'Behold, I the divine being you are experiencing at present am timeless'. But as far as I'm aware, no one has had this type of veridical experience.

[103] I don't mean to suggest that this is an adequate definition of begin, since it is not, and the precise definition of 'begin' is a fraught affair, but rather I use this definition as an example to make my point.

However, PBT might provide some indirect support for the divine being temporal or timeless. For instance, there are thoughts based on *pure* perfections to do with divine knowledge which seem to point in both directions. For instance, we might think that a perfect knower has the best possible justification for their beliefs, which, for events in time, mean being in direct cognitive contact when they occur. But a temporal being cannot be in direct cognitive contact to all events in time, whereas a timeless being can. So, perfect knowledge points in favour of timelessness (Leftow, 1991, 279–280). Nonetheless, we may also think that a perfect knower would know all truths that we have access to, such as truths containing temporal indexical, for instance, having knowledge of what time it is now, but only a temporal being could know these truths, and so this points towards the divine being temporal (Craig, 2001, ch. 4). Thinking about other potential pure perfections like power might also give us indirect evidence for thinking the divine is temporal or timeless, but for ease I'll also ignore these here.

6.2 Is All of This Good Data?

We've seen what some might consider to be data for thinking that the divine is temporal or timeless, but there is an important question to be asked of this data, namely is it any good? That is, since much of the data we have accrued is indirectly relevant, it relies on certain steps before it can provide us with data that is relevant as to whether the divine is temporal or timeless. But it may be that these intermediate steps are faulty and that this supposed data is of no use to our question at all. One job we therefore need to undertake is to evaluate these intermediate steps in order to check the quality of our data.

So, for instance, whilst some have suggested that a timeless being cannot be a person, many have countered this and argued that a timeless being can be a person (e.g. Leftow, 1991, ch. 13; Craig, 2001, ch. 2; Mawson, 2019). Others have contended that time shouldn't be thought of as something creatable (e.g. Swinburne, 2016, 228–231), whilst some have claimed that creation ex nihilo and action in time is perfectly possible for a timeless being (e.g. Page, 2023a; 2025, 53–56; Leftow, 1991, 290–312; forthcoming b). Arguments have also been given to contend that a temporal being can know the future free actions of creatures, or that it's not an issue if it can't (e.g. Craig, 2001, 39–41; Swinburne, 2016, 175–197), whilst others have suggested that a timeless being can consistently undergo *certain types* of change, namely extrinsic changes (Leftow, 1991, 309–312; Page, 2023a, 176–181; 2025, 59–65). This list could continue until it questions all the other indirect reasons we've given for thinking the divine is temporal or timeless, since the steps they require are controversial and disputable. This isn't to suggest that we ultimately shouldn't end up agreeing with some of these steps, since it may be that after considering the arguments for and against them we think that some of the steps are justified. But it is to say that more work will be required on our part in order to determine whether these steps are justified, and it is often the job of philosophy of religion to evaluate these steps. Ultimately, this can allow us to make a more informed decision about what we should count as accurate data for and against the question we are considering.

How good we think the data before us is is therefore something each person will have to judge for themselves. For the purpose of our 'toy' example, let's just value it as follows. Rather than agreeing with Hasker (2002, 137) that the Bible speaks heavily in favour of temporality, or with Leftow (2003; forthcoming b) in thinking that the Bible can be thought of as best supporting the claim that the divine is timeless, I'll side with Crisp (2019, 108) in thinking that biblical data is underdetermined on the question of the divine's relationship to time. In terms of tradition, it's clear that this, at least to some extent, favours timelessness. Regarding experience, let's suppose that this gives us some indirect data in support of temporality. And finally, let's assume that CT gives us some data for timelessness, and that PBT, on the whole, leans towards temporality, since we'll assume that more pure perfections are compatible with temporality than with timelessness.

6.3 Sorting Our Data

We can now sort our 'gerrymandered' data into two groups, with one group supporting temporality, namely experience and PBT, and the other supporting timelessness, namely tradition and CT. Given that we're taking the biblical data to be underdetermined, it would seem that we are left with a draw as to whether the divine is temporal or timeless, with two pieces of data pointing to each view. However, there is more that needs to be considered before making this conclusion.

First, we need to consider the type of data we get from each acquisition method. All the sources other than tradition give us indirect data, since it is data that requires some inferences to be made in order for it to be relevant to our question. Given what I've said previously, I would suggest that we should, all else being equal, prioritise data that is directly relevant more highly than data which is indirectly relevant. As such, we might suppose that the data coming from tradition should be of more epistemic value in determining our model than the data coming from the other acquisition methods, and therefore timelessness will win out. But all else might not be equal. For instance, we might note that traditions can change over time, and something like this seems to be the case when it comes to thinking about the divine's relationship to time, with Leftow claiming that the notion of the divine being temporal now enjoys nearly universal acceptance among philosophers and theologians (1991, 3). Additionally, we might think that the epistemic value of the data given to us by tradition is more generally less valuable than the data we get from other data acquisition methods, say reason, and therefore even though the data of tradition is direct, the indirect data given to us from CT and PBT will still possess more epistemic value.

Supposing we were to think this, it still may be that overall, we should prefer timelessness to temporality, since although the data of reason is to be preferred over other data, it is itself tied, and so we might think the direct data of tradition still trumps the indirect data of experience. But this might also be too fast, for suppose there were a huge number of distinct experiences that various people had of the divine, all of which provided indirect data that the divine was temporal in virtue of it changing. This might tilt the scales to be more balanced, given that eternity isn't explicitly defined as timelessness in the tradition and there are only a handful of cases where it is affirmed. Perhaps we are back to having a tie overall.

But appearances can be deceiving, for if we look more closely at reason, we will realise that it might point more strongly one way rather than the other overall. To see this, note that although PBT may overall point in favour of temporality, it still, we can assume, gives some reasons for thinking the divine is timeless, even if these reasons are weaker than the ones it gives in support of temporality. This may tilt the scales back in favour of timelessness, for if neither CT or PBT should be prioritised, then if CT gives us no reason for thinking that the divine is temporal but some reason to think that the divine is timeless, and PBT gives us some reason to think that the divine is timeless, but more reason to think that it is temporal, we might think that on the whole reason points to the divine being timeless, albeit whilst not providing overwhelming support for this position.

But there's one final thing I've yet to speak about which may throw a spanner into the works, namely our presuppositions. For instance, there are debates in the philosophy of time about what the nature of time is, and it might be that here one has reached the conclusion that time is presentist.[104] However, there is also a fairly widespread thought, albeit contested, that divine timelessness is incompatible with presentism (Craig, 2001, 282),

---

[104] Working out exactly what presentism is happens to be a tricky business (Tallant & Ingram, 2021), but for our purpose let's suppose it just claims that only present things exist.

and so if one finds this claim plausible, given that the data we have doesn't point strongly in favour of timelessness, this might be enough to suggest that we should conclude overall that the divine is temporal.[105]

Our toy model therefore suggests that the divine is temporal.[106] Obviously, when we model the divine more generally things will be much more complicated since there will be more data to deal with, more interconnections between attributes, and more prior commitments to consider. But suppose we've finished constructing our model of the divine, what should we take our model to achieve, and what use will it have? That is the question Section 7 addresses.

7 What Does a 'Divine' Model Actually Give Us?

There is a fairly well-known saying which goes, 'All models are wrong, but some are useful'. If one understands the first part of this statement as claiming that all models are wrong in all respects, then it's surely false, since some models might be partially correct. But if it merely means that models do not fully capture the reality they are attempting to model and therefore they are inadequate in various respects, then this is surely true, even if what they capture is useful. Whatever model of the divine we produce, it too will be inadequate in some respects, although it may nevertheless be useful.

7.1 Keep Calm, It's Just a Model

Now that you've reached the end of this Element, you hopefully possess at least some of the tools required to produce a model of the divine. Yet it's vital to remember that after you've followed this modelling framework what you'll have formulated is a *model* of the divine.[107] This is important as models are *representations*, and not the real things themselves, and one always needs to be on their guard to make sure that they don't substitute

---

[105] See Page (2023b) and Leftow (1991; 2018b; forthcoming b) for some pushback against the claim that timelessness and presentism are incompatible.

[106] Let me just note that before one supposes that this is what *I* actually think, both in terms of what has been said in support of the claim that the divine is temporal or timeless and what we should overall conclude about whether the divine is temporal or timeless, *it isn't*. Rather, everything was deliberately set up in such a way that I could talk about many different judgements one might have to make when modelling. What I actually think is something I'll let remain a mystery.

[107] Much of what I say in this section is meant to address, at least to some degree, contemporary theological concerns about idolatry. For more on this concern and some ways to respond that are compatible with some models of the divine, see Wood (2021, ch. 7).

the thing modelled for the model itself. The model that you will have produced is just a different beast from the thing which is modelled.

This should be especially obvious given what we are attempting to model. After all, even if our model suggests that the divine is omniscient, it clearly would be a mistake to think the *model* was omniscient – rather it is the divine which is omniscient. The model might also claim that the divine is omnipotent, but the *model* isn't omnipotent either, rather the divine is. It would also be a terrible mistake to worship the *model* of the divine, even if our model suggests that the divine is worthy of worship, since it is the divine itself which is to be worshipped. It may well be that the model in some way helps us to think about what the divine is like that is worshipped, providing us with an abstract representation of the divine, but the *model* is not owed any worship.

The distinction is also evident by the fact that models do not perfectly represent that which they model, and so by their nature models may distort, simplify, or idealise reality in some way. But this isn't true of the reality which is modelled. This doesn't imply that some models are better or worse than others, since some might provide a more accurate representation of the reality they are attempting to model when compared with others. But neither model will represent this reality perfectly. Whilst this is true of models more generally, it seems even more likely to be the case when one attempts to model the divine. After all, many take the divine, for some reason or other, to be infinite, and infinite in multiple respects (Göcke & Tapp, 2019). Yet even though my reasoning abilities are good (some might say, first class!), they are nevertheless finite, and so any model of the divine I produce will ultimately be less than what the divine actually is. We might therefore think Plato was right when he said,

> Don't be surprised … if it turns out repeatedly that we won't be able to produce accounts on a great many subjects — on gods … — that are completely and perfectly consistent and accurate. Instead, if we can come up with accounts no less likely than any, we ought to be content, keeping in mind that both I, the speaker, and you, the judges, are only human. So we should accept the likely tale on these matters. It behoves us not to look for anything beyond this. (Timaeus 29b-d, Cooper, 1997, 1235–1236).

Yet this feature of a model, namely that it will be inevitably limited in various ways, should allow us to consider each model and the process itself with humility, since we will be aware that whatever model we are assessing or whatever model we produce, it will be inadequate in capturing the reality we are seeking to represent. Our model of the divine was always going to be deficient in some way, but so too will every other model. If we take the divine to be transcendent, then this no doubt will be something we would have expected from the start, but even if we don't hold this to be an attribute of the divine, out model will nevertheless be insufficient to capture everything of the divine, with this being merely in virtue of what models are able to accomplish. If we suppose we can do better than this, and that we could produce a model which fully captures what the divine is like, we are just confused about the nature of models and ultimately seem to be conflating the reality modelled with the model itself. For to quote Aristotle once again, 'It is the mark of an educated person to look in each area for only that degree of accuracy that the nature of the subject permits' (1094b 24–26, translated by Crisp, 2014, 4–5), and models by their nature only permit so much accuracy. It may therefore be that a model merely allows us to catch a glimmer of what the divine is actually like.[108]

7.2 What Does the Model Give Us?

Given this we might ask what it is that a model actually gives us. One thing we might have thought is that the model tells us something about what the divine nature is actually like, perhaps providing something of a definition of the divine or knowledge of the divine essence. But we don't have to think this. For instance, Aquinas (despite saying that the divine is perfect and good) also claims that we cannot define the divine since the divine cannot be comprehended (*De Potentia Dei*, q.7, a.3, ad 5).[109] Therefore, we might instead suggest that all a model provides us with is language that is appropriate for us to use of the divine, even if it doesn't describe its essence. This is arguably, as Leftow (2004, 143) suggests, all that Anselm sought to achieve when he performed PBT. On this approach, the best we can hope to do, perhaps due to some prior commitment to divine mystery,[110] is to come up with a consistent set of names that are *appropriate* for talking about the divine.

Alternatively, perhaps we think that our model does describe the divine essence. If we go this route then some might worry that we may be subject to the criticism of ontotheology, namely holding that creatures and the divine are ontologically the same, and that this, by its very nature, is

---

[108] Why should we expect to be able to do any more than this, after all, even some scriptures suggest that the divine cannot fully reveal Himself to sinful man without deadly consequences (e.g. Exodus 33:12–23).

[109] See many of the questions between 3 and 25 of *Summa Theologica Prima Pars* for names Aquinas think are appropriate for the divine.

[110] Alston (2005, 100–107) provides some reasons for thinking the divine is mysterious.

Modelling the Divine

theologically objectionable.[111] Yet even if we were to agree that such a stance would be objectionable, our model doesn't need to imply this. For although we might use the same *words* to predicate things of the divine and of creatures, this need not automatically imply that what is predicated is *ontologically* the same in both, or to use the more technical theological terminology, semantic univocity doesn't entail ontological univocity (Wood, 2021, 145–158). Additionally, there's nothing in the method of divine modelling which rules out ontological pluralism, and therefore producing a model of the divine is perfectly compatible with claiming that the divine possesses a different way and degree of being than anything else.[112]

Yet even if we say that our model describes the divine essence, there is a question as to how truly it does so. For instance, in Section 2.2 of the Element I noted that some treat models as mental fictions, but fictions are standardly taken to be those types of things which do not express *literal* truths.[113] This isn't to say that they can't provide very useful information, after all a mathematical fictionalist may claim that mathematics doesn't provide us with literal truths, but they'll no doubt wish to also say that mathematics provides us with very useful fictional information. The same might be true in the divine case, namely that even though our model attempts to describe the divine nature, everything it says will be literally false, albeit useful in various ways.

However, it's not clear that one has to say this, for it does seem that fictional objects may be able to assert truths. For instance, suppose one takes Sherlock Holmes to be a fictional object and yet the truths of mathematics to be objective realist features of the world. When Sherlock utters mathematical truths, it's unclear that we should think that these are literally false in virtue of Sherlock being fictional. Therefore, we might suppose that fictional models can still provide us with some truths.[114] These truths might be 'partial', however this difficult notion is understood, but given that models distort, or simplify, or idealise reality, that the truth they express is 'partial' should be expected. Supposing

---

[111] See Wood (2021, ch. 8) for more on this and some helpful responses.
[112] For a recent defence see McDaniel (2017).
[113] Note that treating a model as a fictional object, such that it has the ontological status of a fictional entity, is another reason for thinking the model and that which is modelled shouldn't be conflated, since whilst the model is a fictional entity, many doing the modelling will think the divine is not.
[114] There is a distinction between *linguistic* fictionalism and *ontological* fictionalism which we might think is at play here, whereby the claim is that an entity can be understood as *ontologically* fictional, whilst their *linguistic* expression doesn't have to be. If it is the case that anything an *ontologically* fictional entity expresses or represents must be fictional too, then the suggestion given above will fail.

that we can make some sense of this notion, then perhaps we should say that when attempting to model the divine, what we attempt to do is say something which at least has the status of being partially true about the divine nature, even if we admit that we will never access the 'whole truth' of the matter.

Our model lacking the ability to say the 'whole truth' may also stem from constraints of language, since the model that we've produced seems compatible with various ways of understanding the language employed to describe the divine.[115] For instance, we might suggest that the language employed is univocal, but equally, it may be that we think analogical language is more appropriate.[116] This may be because of some prior commitment about the divine, or in virtue of numerous data points suggesting that the divine is beyond our comprehension and speech.

It may also be that in our attempt to construct a model of the divine, we find that the task is hopeless, with what is produced being so seemingly contradictory that we either suggest that we should restrict what it is possible to say about the divine, perhaps limiting it to only negations, or suggest that we lack the linguistic or conceptual resources to model the divine.[117] If we take this latter option, we could then either attempt to formulate such resources or perhaps succumb to thinking that the divine is ineffable, and that we would do best to remain silent when thinking about divinity.[118] On this latter approach, we could say that model making is therapeutic, as its failure cures us of the desire to say what cannot be said (Lebens, 2020, 17–28).[119]

7.3 What Is Our Model Useful for?

Let me conclude by briefly saying something about why we might think a model of the divine is useful. Firstly, we might think that it helps to provide us with a more systematic understanding of the divine, rather than leaving us with lots of unruly data points that are yet to be sorted. This

---

[115] See Scott (2013) and Vainio (2020) for a nice introduction to debates about religious language.

[116] Here I use analogy in the way that Aquinas understands it (*Summa Theologica* I, q.13, a.5).

[117] Alternatively, perhaps we should say that this is a reason to think our model can do no better than attempt to achieve a high degree of verisimilitude, rather than truth (Lebens, 2020, 24–28).

[118] The process of trying to produce a model will also be important here, since it will be at least partly through the failure of this process that we come to take this stance on what the divine is like. For some recent analytic work on this type of view see Jacobs (2015).

[119] This might also suggest that what is most important to the divine is personal knowledge of itself rather than propositional knowledge of its nature (Keller, 2018).

Modelling the Divine 61

may ultimately help religious believers better understand and relate to the divine, perhaps in devotional practice, all whilst still acknowledging that the model is distinct from the divine itself and inadequate in various ways. Additionally, it may also help inform one's religious practice, for if one's model informs them that the divine loves them and wishes them to love their fellow man, it may be more likely that they would engage in this praxis.

A model is also useful in showing how different attributes and ideas about the divine interrelate, so that one can clearly see what the connections between different ideas are. Given that it's likely that people will produce substantially different models, seeing the interconnections can also highlight what some of the significant decision points are in model building, as well as showing how various attributes can be arrived at through different means. Additionally, the construction of models will highlight how prioritising certain data acquisition methods can have a determinative effect on our completed model, with much the same being said about one's prior commitments. Ultimately, this will help provide a more fruitful debate between those who produce different models of the divine, since it will make the differences more apparent and clarify what, if anything, can be done about them.

Finally, models are often taken to be useful since they can sometimes be employed to make predictions. It might be that our model can also make predictions, such as stating what a being like the one described in our model is likely or unlikely to do.[120] But even if our model is unable to make predictions, the model may still be useful more generally in debates in philosophy of religion and theology, since often positions taken there are dependent upon the particular model of the divine that one embraces. Models can therefore guide us as to what the most appropriate answers will be to a given question and show us how different answers arise in virtue of adopting different models of the divine.

7.4 Let's Go Model the Divine

As will have been evident from this short Element, there is *much* to think about and consider when attempting to model the divine. It is no easy task, and what will be produced will ultimately be inadequate for fully describing the divine nature. Why then do people engage in modelling the divine, and how confident ought we to be in what we produce? Leftow provides a nice answer when he writes,

---

[120] See Swinburne for some discussion on this (2004, ch.6).

> As a Christian, I am told that where there is knowledge, it will pass away. ... So I work with a guarantee that the best I can do is not good enough and will be obsolete. Why then try to describe God? Some of us just can't wait to open our Christmas present. If my beliefs are true and I explain them well, we may all get a glimpse of it. If my beliefs are false and I explain them well, I still help make the truth better known, as I push others to show where I err. ... Gregory the Great spent long years writing a tome on angels. There is a story that when he got to heaven, he found that he was dead wrong. His reaction? He laughed. I hope someday to react that well. (2000, 145)

So, as you model, do so with a sense of humility, aiming to produce the best model you can, and one which clearly sets out what your data is, how you prioritised it, what your presuppositions were, and how we should understand what it is that your model ultimately claims. Nevertheless, if you are a Christian, you should do so with the knowledge that, 'Now we see a reflection in a mirror; then we will see face-to-face. Now I know partially, but then I will know completely in the same way that I have been completely known' (1 Corinthians 13:12, CEB).[121]

---

[121] This isn't meant to imply that something similar can't be said for other religious traditions, only that the text I cite is authoritative for Christians.

Bibliography

Abdelnour, M. G. (2023) 'The Qur'ān and the Future of Islamic Analytic Theology', *Religions* 14:556. www.mdpi.com/2077-1444/14/4/556.

Adams, R. M. (1999) *Finite and Infinite Goods*. Oxford University Press.

Alston, W. (2005) 'Two Cheers for Mystery!', in A. Dole, & A. Chignell, eds., *God and the Ethics of Belief*. Cambridge University Press, pp. 99–114.

Barth, K. (2020) *Church Dogmatics I.1 The Doctrine of the Word of God*, eds., G. W. Bromiley, & T. F. Torrance. T&T Clark.

Bartholomew, C. G. & Goheen, M. W. (2014) *The Drama of Scripture*, 2nd ed. SPCK.

Beall, J. (2021) *Contradictory Christology*. Oxford University Press.

Beall, J. (2023) *Divine Contradiction*. Oxford University Press.

Bird, M. F. & Harrower, S. (2019) *Trinity without Hierarchy*. Kregel Academic.

Bishop, J. & Perszyk, K. (2023) *God, Purpose and Reality*. Oxford University Press.

Buchak, L. & Zimmerman, D. W. (2022) *Oxford Studies in Philosophy of Religion 10*. Oxford University Press.

Buckareff, A. A. & Nagasawa, Y. (2016) *Alternative Concepts of God*. Oxford University Press.

Byerly, T. R. (2019) 'From a Necessary Being to a Perfect Being', *Analysis* 79:10–17.

Cohoe, C. (2013) 'There Must Be a First', *British Journal for the History of Philosophy* 21:838–856.

Cooper, J. M. (1997) *Plato: Complete Works*. Hackett Publishing.

Craig, W. L. (2001) *God, Time, and Eternity*. Kluwer.

Craig, W. L. & Sinclair, J. D. (2009) 'The kalam Cosmological Argument', in W. L. Craig, & J. P. Moreland, eds., *The Blackwell Companion to Natural Theology*. Wiley-Blackwell, pp. 101–201.

Crisp, R. (2014) *Nicomachean Ethics*. Cambridge University Press.

Crisp, O. (2019) *Analyzing Doctrine*. Baylor University Press.

Cupitt, D. (1980) *Taking Leave of God*. SCM Press.

De Haan, D. (2023) 'Thomist Classical Theism', in J. Fuqua, & R. C. Koons, eds., *Classical Theism*. Routledge, pp. 101–122.

Diller, J. & Kasher, A. (2013) *Models of God and Alternative Ultimate Realities*. Springer.

Dolezal, J. (2011) *God without Parts*. Pickwick Publications.
Doyle, A. C. (2022) *The Complete Sherlock Holmes Collection*. Welbeck Publishing Group.
Dunn, J. D. (1996) *The Epistles to the Colossians and to Philemon*. William B. Eerdmans Publishing Company.
Feser, E. (2009) *Aquinas*. Oneworld Publications.
Frigg, R. & Hartmann, S. (2020) 'Models in Science', in E. N. Zalta, ed., *The Stanford Encyclopedia of Philosophy*. https://plato.stanford.edu/archives/spr2020/entries/models-science/.
Gasser, G. & Kittle, S. (2022) *The Divine Nature: Personal and A-Personal Perspectives*. Routledge.
Giannotti, J. (2021) 'Fundamental Yet Grounded', *Theoria* 87:501–587.
Göcke, B. P. & Tapp, C. (2019) *The Infinity of God*. University of Notre Dame Press.
Gould, P. (2014) *Beyond the Control of God?* Bloomsbury Academic.
Greco, D. (2023) *Idealization in Epistemology*. Oxford University Press.
Hasker, W. (2002) 'Does God Change?', in S. M. Cahn, & D. Shatz, eds., *Questions About God*. Oxford University Press.
Hasker, W. (2010) 'Eternity and Providence', in C. Taliaferro, & C. Meister, eds., *The Cambridge Companion to Christian Philosophical Theology*. Cambridge University Press, pp. 137–145.
Hays, R. B. (1996) *The Moral Vision of the New Testament*. Harper Collins.
Hershtein, L. O. (2023) 'Rethinking Jewish Theology', *Religions* 14:364.
Hill, D. J. (2005) *Divinity and Maximal Greatness*. Routledge.
Huemer, M. (2005) *Ethical Intuitionism*. Palgrave Macmillan.
Jacobs, J. D. (2015) 'The Ineffable, Inconceivable, and Incomprehensible God', *Oxford Studies in Philosophy of Religion* 6:158–176.
Keller, L. J. (2018) 'Divine Ineffability and Franciscan Knowledge', *Research Philosophica* 95:347–370.
Kitcher, P. (1980) 'A Priori Knowledge', *The Philosophical Review* 89:3–23.
Kitcher, P. (2000) 'A Priori Knowledge Revisited', in P. Boghossian, & C. Peacocke, eds., *New Essays on the A Priori*. Oxford University Press, pp. 65–91.
Kopersky, J. (2015) *The Physics of Theism*. Wiley-Blackwell.
Kvanvig, J. L. (2021) *Depicting Deity*. Oxford University Press.
Law, S. (2010) 'The Evil-god Challenge', *Religious Studies* 46:353–373.
Lebens, S. (2020) *The Principles of Judaism*. Oxford University Press.
Leftow, B. (1991) *Time and Eternity*. Cornell University Press.
Leftow, B. (2000) 'A God Beyond Space and Time', in R. A. Varghese, ed., *Theos, Anthropos, Christos*. Peter Lang Publishing, pp. 145–172.

Leftow, B. (2003) 'Scripture, God, and Time', 1st Annual Plantinga Fellow Lecture, March 2003, Notre Dame.
Leftow, B. (2004) 'Anselm's Perfect Being Theology', in B. Davies, & B. Leftow, eds., *The Cambridge Companion to Anselm*. Cambridge University Press, pp. 132–156.
Leftow, B. (2005a) 'The Ontological Argument', in W. J. Wainwright, ed., *The Oxford Handbook of Philosophy of Religion*. Oxford University Press, pp. 80–115.
Leftow, B. (2005b) 'Eternity and Immutability', in W. E. Mann, ed., *The Blackwell Guide to the Philosophy of Religion*. Blackwell, pp. 48–77.
Leftow, B. (2011) 'Why Perfect Being Theology?', *International Journal for Philosophy of Religion* 69:103–118.
Leftow, B. (2012) *God and Necessity*. Oxford University Press.
Leftow, B. (2013) 'God's Deontic Perfection', *Research Philosophica* 90:69–95.
Leftow, B. (2015) 'Perfection and Possibility', *Faith and Philosophy* 32:423–431.
Leftow, B. (2018a) 'Perfect Being Theology and Friendship', in Y. Hazony, & D. Johnson, eds., *The Question of God's Perfection*. Brill, pp. 104–110.
Leftow, B. (2018b) 'Presentism, Atemporality, and Time's Way', *Faith and Philosophy* 35:173–194.
Leftow, B. (2019) 'Infinite Goodness', in B. P. Göcke, &. C. Tapp, eds., *The Infinity of God*. University of Notre Dame Press.
Leftow, B. (2022a) *Anselm's Argument*. Oxford University Press.
Leftow, B. (2022b) 'Perfect Being Attacked!', *Faith and Philosophy* 38:262–273.
Leftow, B. (2023) 'Is Perfect Being Theology Informative?', *Philosophical Quarterly* 73:164–183.
Leftow, B. (2024) 'Conceivability and Perfect Being Theology', *Religious Studies* 60:38–64.
Leftow, B. (forthcoming a) *Perfect Being Theology*.
Leftow, B. (forthcoming b) *Space, Time, and God*. Oxford University Press.
Leftow, B. (in press) 'Perfect Beings and Killer Ghosts', *Oxford Studies in Philosophy of Religion*.
Maclaurin, J. & Dyke, H. (2012) 'What Is Analytic Metaphysics For?', *Australasian Journal of Philosophy* 90:291–306.
Mawson, T. J. (2019) *The Divine Attributes*. Cambridge University Press.
McDaniel, K. (2017) *The Fragmentation of Being*. Oxford University Press.
Miksa, R. (2023) 'From Aesthetic Virtues to God', *TheoLogica* 7:248–273.

Miller, C. (2016) 'Is Theism a Simple Hypothesis?', *Religious Studies* 52:45–61.

Miller, C. (2018) 'The Intrinsic Probability of Theism', *Philosophy Compass* 13:1–12.

Mooney, J. (2019) 'From a Cosmic Fine-tuner to a Perfect Being', *Analysis* 79:449–452.

Murphy, M. C. (2017) *God's Own Ethics*. Oxford University Press.

Murphy, M. C. (2021) *Divine Holiness and Divine Action*. Oxford University Press.

Murphy, M. C. (2023) 'Perfect Goodness', in E. N. Zalta, ed., *The Stanford Encyclopedia of Philosophy*. https://plato.stanford.edu/archives/win2023/entries/perfect-goodness/.

Nagasawa, Y. (2008) 'A New Defence of Anselmian Theism', *Philosophical Quarterly* 58:577–596.

Nagasawa, Y. (2017) *Maximal God*. Oxford University Press.

Ocampo, S. T. (2024) 'Strategies for Stage II of Cosmological Arguments', *International Journal for Philosophy of Religion* 96:55–88.

O'Connor, T. & Montgomery, N. (2013) '*Review: Writing the Book of the World*', *Notre Dame Philosophical Reviews*. https://ndpr.nd.edu/reviews/writing-the-book-of-the-world/.

Oderberg, D. S. (2022) 'Restoring the Hierarchy of Being', in W. M. R. Simpson, R. C. Koons, & J. Orr, eds., *Neo-Aristotelian Metaphysics and the Theology of Nature*. Routledge, pp. 94–124.

Oppy, G. (2013) *The Best Argument against God*. Palgrave Macmillan.

Oppy, G. & Pearce, K. L. (2022) *Is There a God?* Routledge.

Padgett, A. (1992) *God, Eternity, and the Nature of Time*. St Martin's Press.

Page, B. (2019) 'Wherein Lies the Debate? Concerning Whether God Is a Person', *International Journal for Philosophy of Religion* 93:169–188.

Page, B. (2023a) 'The Creation Objection against Timelessness Fails', *International Journal for Philosophy of Religion* 85:297–317.

Page, B. (2023b) 'Presentism, Timelessness, and Evil', *TheoLogica* 7:111–137.

Page, B. (2025) 'Eternal Omni-Powers', *Faith and Philosophy* 41:43–69.

Parsons, T. (1990) 'True Contradictions', *Canadian Journal of Philosophy* 20:335–353.

Paul. L. A. (2012) 'Metaphysics as Modelling', *Philosophical Studies* 160:1–29.

Pawl, T. (2016) *In Defence of Conciliar Christology*. Oxford University Press.

Pawl, T. (2019) *In Defence of Extended Conciliar Christology*. Oxford University Press.

Pawl, T. (2020) 'Conciliar Trinitarianism, Divine Identity Claims, and Subordination', *TheoLogica* 4:102–128.

Plantinga, A. (2000) *Warranted Christian Belief*. Oxford University Press.

Quoteresearch (2015) 'Give a Man a Fish, and You Feed Him for a Day. Teach a Man To Fish, and You Feed Him for a Lifetime', *Quote Investigator*. https://quoteinvestigator.com/2015/08/28/fish/.

Rasmussen, J. (2010) 'Cosmological Arguments from Contingency', *Philosophy Compass* 5:806–819.

Rasmussen, J. (2020) 'An Argument for a Supreme Foundation', in J. Rasmussen, & K. Vallier, eds., *A New Theist Response to the New Atheists*. Routledge, pp. 21–32.

Rasmussen, J. (2024) 'God and Fundamentality', in M. Szatkowski, ed., *Ontology of Divinity*. de Gruyter, pp. 319–331.

Rasmussen, J. & Leon, P. (2019) *Is God the Best Explanation of Things?* Palgrave Macmillan.

Rogers, K. A. (2000) *Perfect Being Theology*. Edinburgh University Press.

Rosen, G. (2010) 'Metaphysical Dependence', in B. Hale, & A. Hoffmann, eds., *Modality: Metaphysics, Logic, and Epistemology*. Oxford University Press, pp. 109–136.

Rubio, D. (2025) 'Intrinsically Good God Created Them', *Oxford Studies in Philosophy of Religion* 11:113–138.

Scott, M. (2013) *Religious Language*. Palgrave Macmillan.

Shields, C. (2024) *Fractured Goodness*. Oxford University Press.

Sider, T. (2011) *Writing the Book of the World*. Oxford University Press.

Speaks, J. (2014) 'The Method of Perfect Being Theology', *Faith and Philosophy* 31:256–266.

Speaks, J. (2018) *The Greatest Possible Being*. Oxford University Press.

Stump, E. (2010) *Wandering in Darkness*. Oxford University Press.

Stump, E. (2023) *Philosophical Theology and the Knowledge of Persons*. Cascade Books.

Swinburne, R. (1994) *The Christian God*. Oxford University Press.

Swinburne, R. (1997) *Simplicity and Evidence of Truth*. Marquette University Press.

Swinburne, R. (2004) *The Existence of God*, 2nd ed. Oxford University Press.

Swinburne, R. (2016) *The Coherence of Theism*, 2nd ed. Oxford University Press.

Tallant, J. & Ingram, D. (2021) 'The Rotten Core of Presentism', *Synthese* 199:3969–3991.

Thomasson, A. L. (2020) 'If Models Were Fictions, Then What Would They Be?', in A. Levy, & P. Godfrey-Smith, eds., *The Scientific Imagination*. Oxford University Press, pp. 51–74.

Titelbaum, M. G. (2012) *Quitting Certainties*. Oxford University Press.

Vainio, O. (2020) *Religious Language*. Cambridge University Press.

van Frassen, B. (1985) 'Empiricism in the Philosophy of Science', in P. Churchland, & C. Hooker, eds., *Images of Science*. University of Chicago Press, pp. 245–308.

Weisberg, M. (2016) 'Modelling', in H. Cappelen, H. S. Gendler, & J. Hawthorne, eds., *The Oxford Handbook of Philosophical Methodology*. Oxford University Press, pp. 262–286.

Williams, T. (2007) *Anselm: Basic Writings*. Hackett Publishing Company.

Williamson, T. (2000) *Knowledge and Its Limits*. Oxford University Press.

Williamson, T. (2022) *The Philosophy of Philosophy*, 2nd ed. Wiley-Blackwell.

Wolter, A. (1987) *Duns Scotus: Philosophical Writings*. Hackett Publishing Company.

Wood, W. (2016) 'Modelling Mystery', *Scientia et Fides* 4:39–59.

Wood, W. (2021) *Analytic Theology and the Academic Study of Religion*. Oxford University Press.

Wright, N. T., & Bird, M. F. (2019) *The New Testament in Its World*. SPCK.

Zagzebski, L. (2017) *Exemplarist Moral Theory*. Oxford University Press.

Zarepour, M. S. (2022) *Necessary Existence and Monotheism*. Cambridge University Press.

Acknowledgements

I've always felt that reading an acknowledgement section is like listening to an acceptance speech at the Oscars. In both, multiple thank-yous are expressed, although undoubtedly not as many as there ought to be, and this will be no different.

The person who deserves the most appreciation for the completion of this project is my wife, Laura. She has repeatedly sacrificed her time so that I could spend more time at work, plugging away at this Element or some other project, and allowed me to skimp out on many of my duties as a husband and father. Her care for our children, Olivia and Jack, has been so great that at times they have barely noticed me gone! But on those occasions where I have been missed, Olivia and Jack have still been very accepting of me leaving playtime early and then asking me how my work has gone once I've returned home. With the Element finished, I'm looking forward to spending more time with each of them (including our third child, Freddie, who was born just before this Element was published). I also want to thank my wider family, who have all been very encouraging whilst I've completed this project and helped us out in numerous ways in order to provide me with the opportunity to get this completed.

There are so many academic colleagues that I could mention who have helped me to get to where I am today. For instance, I owe Bill Mander and Eric Eve a great debt since they took a punt on me when I applied to Harris Manchester College in Oxford to do my BA in Philosophy and Theology after being out of any form of education for a number of years. That experience, along with all the tutors I was lucky enough to have (Sophie Allen, Bill Wood, Tim Mawson, Cecilia Trifogli, Joshua Horden, and Joel Rasmussen), has helped me no end in becoming the thinker I am today. My MPhil tutors (Bill Wood, Brian Leftow, Martin Pickup, Ralph Walker, and Julia Konstantinovsky) and PhD supervisors (Anna Marmodoro and Matthew Tugby) also deserve much thanks in developing my academic ability and interests, such that I'm able to enjoy conducting research on pretty much whatever I fancy thinking about. However, both Brian Leftow and Anna Marmodoro deserve special thanks. Brian has remained, ever since delivering the lectures on philosophy of religion for my BA and supervising my MPhil, a great source of intellectual stimulation and a paradigm that I have sought to emulate when producing work in philosophy of religion (even though this paradigm, much like complete comprehension of God, is not attainable by mere mortals). Anna has been extremely generous to me ever since she first answered my email and agreed to meet to discuss powers and teleology during my first year of undergrad. Since then, she has continually encouraged and helped me with all my philosophical endeavours, being extremely generous with her time, despite her remarkably busy schedule, and always helping improve what I have to say.

Several people deserve specific thanks for either reading large segments of the Element, or discussing various parts of it with me, namely Tim Pawl, Max Baker-Hytch, David Worsley, Sam Lebens, Bill Wood, Tim Mawson, Brian Leftow, and Anna Marmodoro. I feel very lucky to count you all as friends. I also wish to thank Ahnaf Kabir, one of my students at Eton College, who read the whole Element and suggested ways to make it more accessible. Finally, I must thank Michael Peterson, the editor of this series, since he has been *extremely* patient with me, and I hope that he at least thinks the Element was worth the additional two-year wait! (If he, and you my reader, do not think it was, then at least now you all know who my teachers were, and can blame them!)

Cambridge Elements

The Problems of God

Series Editor
Michael L. Peterson
Asbury Theological Seminary

Michael L. Peterson is Professor of Philosophy at Asbury Theological Seminary. He is the author of *God and Evil* (Routledge); *Monotheism, Suffering, and Evil* (Cambridge University Press); *With All Your Mind* (University of Notre Dame Press); *C. S. Lewis and the Christian Worldview* (Oxford University Press); *Evil and the Christian God* (Baker Book House); and *Philosophy of Education: Issues and Options* (Intervarsity Press). He is co-author of *Reason and Religious Belief* (Oxford University Press); *Science, Evolution, and Religion: A Debate about Atheism and Theism* (Oxford University Press); and *Biology, Religion, and Philosophy* (Cambridge University Press). He is editor of *The Problem of Evil: Selected Readings* (University of Notre Dame Press). He is co-editor of *Philosophy of Religion: Selected Readings* (Oxford University Press) and *Contemporary Debates in Philosophy of Religion* (Wiley-Blackwell). He served as General Editor of the Blackwell monograph series Exploring Philosophy of Religion and is founding Managing Editor of the journal *Faith and Philosophy*.

About the Series
This series explores problems related to God, such as the human quest for God or gods, contemplation of God, and critique and rejection of God. Concise, authoritative volumes in this series will reflect the methods of a variety of disciplines, including philosophy of religion, theology, religious studies, and sociology.

Cambridge Elements

The Problems of God

Elements in the Series

God and Happiness
Matthew Shea

God and the Problem of Epistemic Defeaters
Joshua Thurow

The Problem of God in Jewish Thought
Jerome Gellman With Joseph (Yossi) Turner

The Trinity
Scott M. Williams

The Problem of Divine Personality
Andrew M. Bailey and Bradley Rettler

Religious Trauma
Michelle Panchuk

Embodiment, Dependence, and God
Kevin Timpe

The Problem of God in Thomas Reid
James Foster

God and Non-Human Animals
Simon Kittle

Divine Motivation and Humanity
Jordan Wessling and Ross Parker

God and Technology
Heidi A. Campbell

Modelling the Divine
Ben Page

A full series listing is available at: www.cambridge.org/EPOG

Made in the USA
Monee, IL
03 May 2026

49437533R00046